THE PIVOT PRINCIPLE

WHEN CHANGING DIRECTION HAPPENS:

FIVE DAILY HABITS NEEDED TO MANAGE CHANGE, SLAY CHAOS, AND CREATE LASTING PEACE

WRITTEN BY

DR. O. SHELLEY KEMP,

ED.D., SHRM-SCP

Published by hope*books
2217 Matthews Township Pkwy
Suite D302
Matthews, NC 28105
www.hopebooks.com

hope*books is a division of hope*media

Printed in the United States of America

First paperback edition.
Paperback ISBN: 979-8-89185-314-0
Hardcover ISBN: 979-8-89185-315-7
Ebook ISBN: 979-8-89185-316-4
Library of Congress Number: 2025944921

hb
hope*books

TABLE OF CONTENTS

What Fans are Saying About *The PIVOT Principle*

"As someone who's had to pivot more than once when life didn't go as planned, this book hit home. Shelley doesn't just talk about the PIVOT Routine, she lived it. And reading her story reminded me that every setback can lead to something greater if you're willing to shift. The PIVOT Principle is real, practical, and honest. If you're in the middle of a transition or trying to find your footing again, this book feels like someone walking beside you saying, 'You've got this.'"

—Cam F Awesome

12-time National Champion Heavyweight Olympic Boxer and Former Captain of Team USA Boxing; Keynote Speaker; Author of *Becoming Awesome: How to Make Success Inevitable*

"Dr. Kemp's The PIVOT Principle *drew me in from the very first chapter. This is more than a book—it is a roadmap for those overwhelmed by life's chaos and unsure where to begin again. Rooted in prayer, it guides readers to rediscover hope, dreams, confidence, and the assurance that their story is far from over. This book will help you make the right pivot—one that draws you closer to God, strengthens your family, and renews your sense of purpose."*

—Charles Daniels Jr.

Founder & Senior Pastor, The Truth Church, Memphis, TN

"What I appreciate about The Pivot Principle *is its honesty. Shelley doesn't just talk about change — she shares her story. Her framework is simple and straightforward, offering encouragement and practical tools for those moments when life feels uncertain."*

—Brad Federman

CEO, Performance Point, LLC., Culture & Leadership Development Expert; Author of *Never Delegate Again: Uncover the Secret of Growing your Company, Your People, and Yourself*

"Dr. Kemp has done a remarkable job showing us what it means to pivot when life's storms hit. Whether facing adversity in our personal or professional lives, we are all called to pivot— and she invites us into that process with honesty and grace. Through her powerful story—both professional and deeply personal, including her son's accident—and her unwavering faith in God, she offers a real-time, relatable, and daily practice for PIVOTing through change. This book is a must-read for every leader who leads with faith at their core, who seeks continued growth, and who understands that sometimes, the most courageous move we can make is to pivot."

—Dr. Will Lewis, MSW, Ph.D.

Author of *Sweet Potato Pie vs Pumpkin Pie* and *Perched in the Storm: How Resilient Entrepreneurs Rise;* Co-Founder, The Intersection

"In The Pivot Principle, *Shelley delivers a blueprint on navigating change with grace, grit, and God's wisdom. Shelley*

invites us to embrace every pivot not as a setback, but as a sacred setup that prepares us for what's next. The Pivot Principle *is a compass for your journey through uncertainty to possibility. Whether you're shifting careers, relationships, or mindset, Shelley's heart in book form, will leave you empowered to rise, realign, and live with hope and purpose."*

—Loretta McNary

Award-Winning Media Host of *The Loretta McNary Show*, CEO and Transformation Coach, McNary Media; Author of *Live Like You Believe*

"This isn't just a book. It's a lifeline disguised as a playbook. In The Pivot Principle, *Dr. Shelley Kemp doesn't just share a powerful testimony—she gifts us a daily rhythm for resilience. Whether you're navigating heartbreak, a health crisis, a career change, or just the everyday grind of being human, this book will meet you there—with honesty, wisdom, and a practical plan to move forward. This isn't about hype or hustle. It's about healing. And this book will walk with you through the work of it—five minutes at a time. If you're looking for clarity, hope, or a practical way to change your life—start here."*

—Melissa Jean Rod

Author of *The Daddy Files* & Collaborative Author of *Anchored in Hope*

"For a number of years now I have been fascinated about how people successfully approach change and navigate transitions, especially unexpected and unwanted change. I've also been drawn to a number of theories and concepts about change,

but even moreso, I'm drawn by their practical application, because that is where real transformation happens. In her book, The Pivot Principle: When Changing Directions Happen, *Dr. Kemp intertwines both —the principle and the practical. That is why this book is a must read. Master the art of the pivot by applying the wisdom contained herein."*

—Gwendolyn J. Tucker

President, RIX International; Leadership & Talent Development Strategist; Author of *Called to Lead: What to Do When a Leadership Position Finds You*

To Anthony –

Watching you reinvent yourself gave me
the language for this message.
I would not be me if there was no you.
I love you.

To Andre –

Your strength gave this book its heartbeat.
Your quiet strength steadies me.
You make me better every single day.
I love you.

Thank you both for showing me how to
pivot with purpose, grace, and faith.

ACKNOWLEDGEMENTS

They say it takes a village to raise a child—well, it also takes a village to write a book. This project wasn't born in isolation; it was shaped, stretched, and strengthened by the people God placed beside me. From the encouragers who reminded me to keep writing, to the truth-tellers who offered real feedback when I needed it most, and the quiet warriors who simply showed up during moments of doubt—you helped bring *The PIVOT Principle* to life. Thank you for walking with me, praying for me, and believing in this message even before it was fully formed. I couldn't have done this without you.

Andre – Yes, my dear husband, I am thanking everyone! But you are tops. You are the greatest love I have ever known. You make every dream come true. I may be too independent at times, but there is no me without you. I can stand tall because of you. I love you.

Anthony – my son, my greatest accomplishment, my greatest gift. I am a much better person in this world because you are here. This story was actually yours to tell, so I cannot thank you enough for allowing me to put words on paper. This pivot was tragic, yes. But only YOU could have handled it with such resiliency, such patience. I am so proud of you. You have turned lemons into the sweetest lemonade. You are the best part of me. I know God has such great plans for your future. Trust Him. Lean into Him. I love you.

Missy – my *oldest* friend (well, that's what she calls me... *old*), my self-selected sister, and my best friend. We have been friends for more than 50 years, and it's amazing that she never grew tired of me following her around when we were kids. I would not have cared if she had, because she was my bestie, and I was determined to stay in her life. Missy, I am so proud of you. Here we are, both authors, both with families, traveling and impacting others with our stories. Thank you for checking in on me when we go months without a word to each other because of our schedules. Thank you for sending me cards in the mail that affirmed I still mattered to you. Thank you for your annual Christmas cards that updated me on everything that was happening with all of your kids. Thank you for inviting me on weekend trips to recharge, and thank you for saying "yes" each time I would purchase two concert tickets before asking if you were available to travel. You are living proof that God gives great gifts to His children.

Susan – my dear friend, another self-selected sister, and my best friend through so many of life's pivot moments. You are so strong. You have so much untapped strength. Thank you for keeping me lifted, for encouraging me, and for reminding me of all the things I have forgotten over the years.

Ruth – my cheerleader, my sister-in-Christ, and my ex-mother-in-love. I'm convinced there would not have been a Dr. Shelley Kemp, emphasis on the doctor, if it hadn't been for Ruth. It is because of this woman that I went back to college at the age of 30 to complete my bachelor's degree at Crichton College in Memphis, Tennessee. And then my master's at Central Michigan University. And then my doctorate at Liberty University. Other than my parents, she was the first to see my potential. And what's even greater than seeing one's potential is speaking that potential to life. That's what she did for me. Thank you for supporting me for the last 25 years.

Essence, Kennedy, Cameron, and Tyler – to the sweet family that adopted me for five months. Thank you for embracing me, for allowing me to be your Secret Santa, and for being a beautiful example of a strong and supportive family unit.

To my Beta Readers, Ella, Charlene, Carrie, Angelica, Michael, Theresa, Tanika, Kim, Sara Beth, Bridget, and Lisa – Y'all! As my beta readers, you were so wonderful! I cannot thank you enough for trusting me, for being so transparent and honest with your feedback. I cannot imagine completing this book project without you. Your words of encouragement were so affirming. Your suggestions for improvements, additions, or deletions were so enlightening and impactful.

Loretta – How do I put a title on who you are to me? Friend, yes. Mentor, yes. Greatest Master Mind Leader, absolutely! Science shows that to be casual friends, you have to speak 40-60 hours with a person. A true friendship requires 80-100 hours. Close friends, however, require over 200 hours of intentional, quality interactions. You, my dear friend, have poured into me without my asking. You have encouraged me, challenged me, and corrected me. I am so glad we continued to cross paths over the years until we finally surrendered and became true friends. May God bless you and your ministry. May everything you touch prosper, glorify God, and provide a graceful covering to those in need.

Carolyn MB – the Queen! I am so glad we connected through Loretta. As the founder and CEO of A Tour of Possibilities (ATOP) in Memphis, I am amazed at your heart for people and history. May God bless you and your marketplace ministry. May everything you touch prosper, glorify God and provide a safe space for those in need.

Diana - My Spiritual Sister, Mindful Mentor, and my friend! We have been on similar journeys, and our monthly meet-ups—those encouragement and prayer sessions—were everything I never knew I needed in life. God was so faithful when He introduced me to you in Kansas City.

Brian, Hope, Carrie, Angela, Amanda – my publisher, publishing partner, my coach, my developmental editor, and copy assistant. This book became what it is because of your guidance and patience with me. I know I want *all the things,* and I want them all now, but you had the patience to guide me through this process. And those first edits? Angela! It's as if your feedback unlocked exactly what I needed to polish my little gem. I am so thankful God placed you in my life at the exact moment I needed you. Amanda, how do you do what you do? You are amazing! Thank you.

To Our Winding Path Women's Club, honorably MJ, Sandie, Dena, Cindy, Cindy, Krista, Rachel, Tonia, Patsy, Kim, Sherri, Donna, Shellie, Karissa, Becky, Theresa, Tammy, Laura, Shonna, Kassie, Susan, Jennifer – my tribe! MJ gave us all a huge blessing by putting us together online. Someone once told me that there are souls attached to our obedience. I believe that MJ's obedience to start this online group, so many years ago, provided us all with blessings we never would have experienced otherwise. I'm so thankful for each of you. While I wish we were closer in proximity, I always look forward to seeing your notifications come through my phone with those daily check-ins. Thank you all for supporting me. Next—let's plan a book tour to everyone's city!

FOREWORD

By Dianna Jackson, LCSW

I first met Shelley three years ago during a six-month Mindfulness Certification training. From our very first retreat, something clicked—and we've been connected ever since. Over countless breakfasts and brainstorming sessions that followed, a meaningful friendship and sisterhood took root—one built on shared vision, mutual encouragement, and a deep desire to grow personally, professionally, and spiritually. To this day, those morning meetings continue to inspire and sharpen us as we walk alongside one another in faith and purpose.

Shelley is a woman of virtue and great faith. She is full of life, purpose, and resilience. Insightful, ambitious, and tenacious, she encourages others with unwavering authenticity. She is, without a doubt, a Godsend. Over the years, I've had the joy of witnessing her grow—not only in her walk with God, but also in her many roles as an entrepreneur, trainer, writer, speaker, and cherished friend.

The PIVOT Principle: Five Daily Habits Needed to Manage Change, Slay Chaos, and Create Lasting Peace has truly blessed me. Not only is it beautifully written—it's also deeply inspiring. Shelley speaks with a transparency and vulnerability that many shy away from. And why is that? Because challenges and change are rarely easy. They disrupt our sense of control, stretch our emotional limits, and stir up fears of inadequacy. Let's be honest—not many of us are lining up for that kind of ride.

And yet, that's exactly why this book is so powerful—and so timely.

In a world marked by constant change—whether in our relationships, careers, personal growth, or spiritual lives—this book offers practical, faith-filled guidance to help us navigate the unexpected with grace and resilience.

Drawing from her own transformative journey, Shelley uncovers a life-changing truth: the key to lasting success isn't found in grand, sweeping gestures—but in small, consistent, intentional actions. Through *The PIVOT Principle*, she teaches us how five simple daily practices, done in just five minutes a day, can shift our mindset—from survival to strength, from victim to victor, from panic to peace.

What I love most is that Shelley reminds us we don't have to start from scratch. Chances are, many of us are already practicing at least one or two of these steps. But in this book, she shows us how combining all five—like the perfect five-ingredient recipe—can unlock resilience and peace in powerful ways. Each step is helpful on its own, but together? Game-changer. Talk about an "aha" moment!

This book is a must-read. It offers clarity and courage for whatever season you're in. And if you're holding it now, know this: you're in the right place. Whether you're navigating uncertainty, feeling stuck, or simply seeking a more grounded way to live, *The PIVOT Principle* will meet you there. Shelley is the real deal—wise, grounded, and anointed for this moment. Trust her voice. Trust the process. And most of all, trust that what's ahead of you is worth the pivot.

Enjoy!

COACH'S INTRODUCTION: WHAT AND WHY A GOOD PIVOT MATTERS

et's face it: change happens.

It happens to everyone, and it is an inevitable fact happening with or without us even knowing about it, wanting it, creating it, or forcing it to occur.

Divorce.

An unwanted medical diagnosis.

Pregnancy.

Miscarriage.

Empty nesting.

Promotion.

Downsizing.

Rightsizing.

Upskilling.

Reskilling.

Retirement.

Lifestyle changes. Family changes. Marital changes. Physical changes.

People write books about change. Change management. Change agents. Change movements. Change theories.

Change. Change. Change.

Society loves to categorize it, too—social change, political change, demographic change, climate change. Even religious organizations initiate change for both members and non-members. Revivals. Conferences. Global summits.

With all of this talk about change, I completely underestimated how much it would affect me—despite my best efforts to control so many aspects of my life and my family's. I've always been intentional. I never just had a Plan A or B; I had plans C, D, and E lined up, too. I wanted my life to look like the standard married professional: a spouse, one kid, one dog, two cars, and a home on a cul-de-sac. Instead, I became the prodigal daughter—privileged, sheltered, and selfish in youth. Then a two-time divorcée, an ex–wannabe fitness queen, and eventually, a single mom. I thought life would simply flow and carry me to the same spot my parents reached by my age: standing at the top of a respected career, weighing retirement plans, thinking about travel, grandkids, more work, or all three—until the end.

But that's not how it went.

The changes I've lived through haven't led me to the pinnacle of my career, or to the luxury of deciding how many more years I'll work, or whether to spend retirement raising grandbabies or boarding planes. After a second divorce, dating in my 40s, and finally finding success on my own, life eventually got sweet again. I remarried—this time to someone I trust to keep me grounded and safe, even as life keeps shifting.

I'm still intentional. But now, I view change differently.

Change doesn't just happen to me.

Change happens *for* me.

I can embrace it, manage it, or move past it—but either way, I stay in control when change shows up. And this is what I want for you! I want you to view change differently. It's not something that happens to you, good or bad. That career change you're facing right now? That's not happening because you necessarily did something wrong. The change you're feeling is really a misalignment, and whatever is happening right now that's making you change directions, it's for your benefit. Or that relationship that's weighing you down or causing you to wonder what's wrong with you? That's another misalignment. Sure, there may be areas where you can accept responsibility, learn something, or grow, but when we are misaligned in our careers, our relationships, or our mission, changes often occur so that we can find alignment. So that we can return to our most productive selves. So that we can escape all the chaos and anxiety of a misaligned life and instead experience a calm, joyful, and peaceful life.

How does that sound?

Want to know how I do it?

I picture change like a pivot on a basketball court.

(Now don't check out on me! You may not be a basketball fan—but neither was I. And yet, here we are, talking about one of the most classic moves in the game. Stick with me.)

Before 1999, pivot was just a straightforward, two-syllable word that meant to turn or to shift direction while staying rooted. But thanks to a now-famous *Friends* episode—where Ross yells "PIVOT!" while trying to wedge a couch up a stairwell—it became a pop culture punchline, plastered across memes, mugs, and T-shirts everywhere. But allow me to introduce a broader perspective—one that comes from a mother's point of view and a late-blooming fan of the sport of basketball..

Early Lessons from Basketball

My son has always loved basketball. He loved playing it, watching it, dreaming about it, and even planning a future with it. From the moment he first held a basketball, I could see the spark in his eyes—a fire that ignited every time he touched the ball. As his mom, I've grown to love everything it means to our household—tryouts, practices, season openers, weekend games, over-the-top parents yelling at refs, tournaments, the buzzer. Oh, I love the buzzer. You don't hear the buzzer in baseball or football. Just basketball. It's that final, electrifying sound that marks a moment of victory or defeat, but always with intensity. Every time I hear it, it brings back memories of all those early mornings and late nights spent at gyms, the anticipation in the air, the sweat on his brow, and the cheers of parents—some louder than others.

He played three sports as a kid, football, baseball, and basketball, but basketball—basketball has always been his heartbeat. It's where he found his true passion, his rhythm. And for me, it became more than just a sport we shared. Basketball gave us years of conversation—about fairness, teamwork, discipline, and what it means to win and lose with grace. We've had long talks about the lessons learned on and off the court—how each win is built on teamwork, and each loss is an opportunity to learn.

Now, more than fifteen years later, those lessons still come up in our home. They're not just memories; they're part of the fabric of our daily lives. Basketball has shaped the way we approach challenges, work together, and find joy in the process. It's given us something else to share, a reason to celebrate, and a way to grow together—not just as a family, but as individuals. The lessons we learned on the court have been our foundation during times of change. And though Anthony's love for basketball is as strong as ever, it's these lessons that have stayed with us through the years.

And still, after all those years of sitting in the bleachers, I never fully understood the value of the pivot. Well, more specifically, the pivot foot.

After more than 15 years as a basketball parent and six years working in the National Basketball Association (NBA), I eventually picked up the jargon of the game. Most people are familiar with the dribble, lay-up, rebound, and jump shot. But the pivot? That's the move that often gets overlooked, yet it's the one that has the potential to teach anyone more about how to approach life than they ever expected.

Time-out: If you are a basketball player, coach, or fan, please know that my explanations for on-court vernacular are going to be VERY loose. Take no offense, please. I'm appealing to those who aren't as basketball-savvy as you.

The pivot is a fundamental skill in basketball that plays a crucial role in a player's ability to navigate the court effectively. One, the pivot allows players to maintain control of the ball while changing direction. Two, as players pivot, they can set up better passing angles and shooting positions. This helps when players attempt passes and set up clear shots. Third, the pivot helps players protect the ball from defenders, making it harder for the defender to steal the ball. Pivots help with a player's agility and flexibility. Not only do pivots enhance a player's agility, but they also allow players to make sharp turns and quick movements. If you've ever watched a basketball game, you know that points are made when players can demonstrate their agility and flexibility. So, mastering the art of the pivot can significantly improve a player's overall performance on the court.

But the pivot isn't just about the game. It's a metaphor for life.

Imagine this: You're playing in the final seconds of a tied game. The ball is in your hands. The clock is ticking down, and the crowd is holding its breath. You start moving forward, but you're quickly surrounded by defenders. The easy shot isn't there anymore, and you feel like the game might slip away. This is where the pivot comes in. Rather than forcing a bad shot or losing possession, you plant one foot and pivot—shifting your direction with precision. Now, instead of being stuck, you've created a new angle, a new opportunity to pass, shoot, or dribble your way toward success. In that split second, you've made the right decision, stayed calm, and turned what looked like a failure into a chance to win the game.

Life often feels like those last few seconds—like everything is coming at you all at once, and you must act fast. But just like in basketball, you don't always need to make a dramatic move. Sometimes, the best decision is to stay grounded, assess your options, and pivot in a new direction. Maybe you don't need to leave your current position in life or career completely; sometimes a shift in perspective or approach is all it takes to find the right path.

By mastering the pivot, you learn how to stay in control when everything seems chaotic, how to adjust when circumstances change, and how to create new opportunities even when the ones you expected to come your way are blocked. That's the power of the pivot—and it's something you can apply every day, both on and off the court.

In this next section, I want you to visualize a basketball player—it can be your favorite player like Kobe, Jordan, Curry, or Morant, or it can be your kid. This part is so important to understand *The PIVOT Principle* because the mechanics of what happens on court is so amazing when you start applying it to your everyday routine. So, keep going!

How Players Execute a PIVOT

Step One: *Establish the Pivot Foot*

When a player catches the ball, they must decide which foot will serve as the pivot foot. This foot is the one that remains planted on the court while the other foot is free to move. The pivot foot must be solidly grounded to create a strong foundation for the next move.

Step Two: *Get Into the Triple Threat Position*

This position is a fundamental aspect of basketball. It's an offensive stance that gives players several options for their next move. From the triple threat position, a player can either pass, shoot, or dribble the ball. When you're on the court, you always want to have multiple options. The triple threat position provides just that, keeping the defense guessing while the player is in control.

Step Three: *Consider the Direction in Which You Want to Go*

Once the pivot foot is established, the player must decide whether to move forward or backward.

Forward Pivot: If the player chooses to move forward, they keep the pivot foot planted and step forward with the non-pivot foot. A forward pivot helps create more space and better angles for passing and shooting, enabling a clearer path to scoring.

Reverse Pivot: If the player opts to move backward, they keep the pivot foot planted and step backward with the non-pivot foot. A reverse pivot is useful for protecting the ball from defenders and creating more time to make the next move.

Step Four: *Find and Maintain Your Balance*

After the pivot, it's crucial for the player to regain their balance. The pivot foot must remain firmly grounded on the court. If a player lifts, slides, or moves the pivot foot before passing, dribbling, or shooting the ball, they will be called for a traveling violation. Maintaining balance ensures that the player remains in control and able to make the next move effectively.

Step Five: *Use Your Body*

As you pivot, use your body to shield the ball from defenders. This maneuver helps the player maintain control, creating space and protecting the ball from a steal. The player's body becomes a barrier, further emphasizing the importance of using both physicality and agility in executing the pivot.

Bonus Tip: Great players practice pivoting with both feet. This versatility allows them to be unpredictable and difficult to defend against, making them far more effective on the court. By mastering pivots from both feet, players can adapt to a variety of situations and keep their opponents on edge.

What If We Applied the Pivot Principles to Our Lives?

By now, you've seen how the pivot works on the court— how a player uses a planted foot to remain steady while scanning the floor for the next best move. But let's zoom out. What if we brought those same principles into our everyday lives? Into our careers, our relationships, our families, our faith, or even our mindset?

Here's the truth: you and I are pivoting all the time— whether we recognize it or not. Every unexpected phone call, hard conversation, job change, or parenting challenge is a moment where we can either freeze up or ground ourselves and move with purpose.

As we move into the next chapter, consider how these seven principles of a great pivot on the court also apply to real life:

- **A pivot requires action.** You can't stay stuck. Progress requires decisions—imperfect or not. When life shifts, you must shift too.

- **A pivot needs a solid foundation.** Just like an athlete establishes a pivot foot, you need values, vision, and goals you can stand on when the world around you gets shaky.

- **The triple-threat position gives you options.** On the court, it prepares you to pass, shoot, or drive. In life, it's about preparing your mind, your schedule, and your heart for more than one path forward.

- **A pivot is an intentional movement.** You're not spinning in circles—you're choosing direction. Sometimes it's a step forward; other times it's a pause or even a step back to reset. It all counts when it's intentional.

- **A player protects the ball or creates space.** You protect what matters—your peace, your relationships, your dreams. A good pivot helps you hold on to your priorities while carving out room to breathe and grow.

- **A pivot requires recalibration.** You don't just move and hope it works. You pause, rebalance, and make sure you're still headed toward the goal. Life's pivots are the same—requiring alignment, not chaos.

- **Pivots must be practiced.** You won't get good at changing direction overnight. But the more you train your body, mind, and spirit to respond with clarity and resilience, the smoother your pivots become.

You don't need a jersey to apply pivots. You just need the willingness to ground yourself and move—on purpose. Let's move into the next chapter and explore how this looks, step by step.

Now that you've seen how the pivot works on the court—rooted, intentional, and strategic—let me take you to the year that redefined that word for me entirely. The year was 2018. That year, everything changed.

Not only did I leave a job where I was loved, valued, and repeatedly asked to stay—I also stepped into what I thought was my dream job: working as a Human Resource (HR) Manager for an NBA team. It was everything I had worked for, everything I had prayed for, everything I thought would fulfill me. And yet, even with the dream job came pressure, expectation, and a level of stress I hadn't fully anticipated. In that moment, I realized that even the most well-thought-out dreams don't always come with the peace and satisfaction we expect.

And then came the accident.

The moment everything else faded into the background. The moment when basketball, titles, and career wins no longer mattered. What happened in 2018 redefined success for me. It reframed how I approach my faith, my family, my work, and my wellness.

It was in that moment of crisis that I began to understand the true power of the pivot—not just on the basketball court, but in life. Sometimes, to truly move forward, we must pause, pivot, and change our direction in ways we never expected.

That's the year *The PIVOT Principle* was born. It wasn't born in a classroom, a boardroom, or on the court. It was born in the messy, uncertain, and vulnerable moments when I had no choice but to make a shift—to make a pivot— that would change the course of my family's life.

As we move into the next chapter, I invite you to consider: What would it look like if you embraced the pivot in your own life? What might happen if you began to reframe success and see the moments of challenge and change as opportunities to grow, learn, and ultimately pivot toward something greater?

Just like a basketball game, this book is divided into two halves. The first half walks you through each fundamental step of a strong, strategic PIVOT—laying the groundwork for personal growth, resilience, and purpose. The second half shows you how to bring it all together by applying the PIVOT as a repeatable daily routine—whether in your work, your relationships, or your wellness. One half is your training: the other, your real-time execution. Together, they form a playbook you can return to again and again— whenever life calls for a new direction.

Reminder from Coach Shelley

Life won't wait until you feel ready. It presses in—fast and full court—just when you think you've caught your breath. But the goal isn't to outrun the pressure; it's to plant your feet, hold your position, and pivot through it with clarity, courage, and consistency.

The PIVOT Principle isn't about perfection or instant wins. It's about developing a daily rhythm that keeps you steady when everything else is in motion. Whether you're dealing with a job change, relationship conflict, grief, or just the ache of not knowing what's next —this playbook gives you five daily habits to help you move forward with bold, focused action.

You don't need the perfect game plan to begin. You just need to show up, stay grounded, and make the next right move.

Let's build a life that doesn't crumble under pressure.
Let's pivot with purpose.

FIRST HALF

THE STORY BEHIND THE PIVOT

"WHEN I SAID, 'MY FOOT IS SLIPPING,'
YOUR LOVE, LORD, SUPPORTED ME.
WHEN ANXIETY WAS GREAT WITHIN ME,
YOUR CONSOLATION BROUGHT ME JOY."
—PSALM 94:18-19

The Accident

2018 was the year I finally made it to the NBA. It was almost six weeks out from the season opener, and I had been hired as the HR Manager for the Memphis Grizzlies. During my third week with the Grizzlies, at precisely 5:26 pm, I received a text:

Come home.

Now.

Anthony.

Accident...

Lawnmower

That is all I got. Come home. Now. Anthony. Accident. Moments later, that final one-word explanation, "lawnmower," flashed.

❊ ❊ ❊

Anthony was two years old the first time I put a basketball in his hands.

The ball was bigger than his head, and I knew he wouldn't be able to dribble or get it into the preschool-sized hoop I'd bought from Toys-R-Us. That didn't matter. I just wanted him to feel it—the bounce of the rubber, the texture of the pebbled grip, the smell of fresh leather.

I wasn't a basketball player.

But I'd always wanted to be.

It was seventh grade when tryouts were announced at Alice Johnson Jr. High. I was so excited—this would be my first chance to finally be part of a team. I practiced every day in our driveway in Channelview, Texas, a small suburb outside Houston. The heat was relentless, but I didn't care. I had circled the tryout date on our tiny refrigerator calendar from the bank. It was everything.

Tryouts were scheduled for Tuesday. My mom planned to leave work early to pick me up, but when I got home from school, I called her.

"Mom, Miss Pendergrass said they moved tryouts to next week. You don't have to leave early. I'm going outside to practice."

I was still excited—I had one more week to get better.

Next Tuesday arrived. I headed to the girls' gym, bag in hand, ready to change. A different coach saw me walking in.

"Where are you going?" she asked.

"To dress out for tryouts," I said.

She frowned.

"Tryouts were last Thursday. You missed them. That's rule number one—you've gotta show up. Maybe next year."

I stood there, stunned. My heart sank. Had Miss Pendergrass given me the wrong date on purpose? Had I misunderstood?

I missed my bus that day. Sat alone for three hours until my mom could pick me up. When she arrived, she saw my face before I could say a word. "You didn't make it?" she asked gently. "No," I whispered. "They held tryouts last week. I missed them. Coach said I can try again next year."

And then I cried. Again.

I was devastated. Did I mishear? Or had someone made sure I wouldn't show up?

Now, nearly forty years later, I still think about that moment—my one shot. The date that got "moved." The tears. The ride home.

Coach was wrong.

I never tried out again.

Anthony loved to play basketball. He was the youngest player on the Junior Grizzlies church league when he was 4-going-on-5 years old. They were so cute in their oversized jerseys and shorts. Anthony insisted on wearing a headband, too. Adorable. Every year, he tried out, and every year, he made it. They didn't have school teams until the seventh grade, but by the time seventh grade came around, he had already accumulated eight years of court time, four championships, three team leader awards, eight MVP awards, and two Player-of-the-Year awards. Basketball was life.

At fifteen years old, Anthony lived and breathed basketball. Like me, he wasn't on the team at school either. No, he didn't miss tryouts. Instead, we moved to a different city, and the coaches in our new town didn't know Anthony. They hadn't seen him play like they had seen the other boys in school play. By high school, Anthony had become a generous player, too. While he started out as a ball-hogger, he amped up his passing game in his early teens. At tryouts, his passing game wasn't appreciated on the court. He never made the team in our new town. When they called out the last person chosen for the team in his seventh-grade year, I was capturing him on videotape, and I accidentally got his reaction. I will never forget his face when they did NOT call his name. A parent never wants to see their child in pain, physical, emotional, or otherwise. His best friend, Jaron, put his arm around him and gave him some words of encouragement. That day was rough. He never tried out for a school team ever again.

Instead, he continued playing in church and community leagues.

He was fifteen years old. Confident. Friendly to others. Generous. Kind. Funny, with a great sense of humor. He wasn't on a team, but he appreciated how basketball brought kids together who would never have otherwise known one another. Basketball was still life.

I couldn't stop thinking about the cryptic text. I ran to my car. I still cannot remember how I got from the employee garage to the freeway, but somehow, I found myself on the freeway headed toward the house 35 minutes away. I turned the radio off and started talking to God. Even if a mother did not believe in God, I would suspect that in this situation, she might start praying to a deity whom she had never met, never heard, never seen, and never experienced before just to ensure all her bases were covered as she hurried to her only son. For me, though, I knew Him. God was not an abstract idea to me. Our relationship was very personal and had been growing over the last fifteen years. Sitting in my car driving home, I knew I was wearing the full armor Paul talks about in Ephesians, everything from the helmet of salvation on my head to the shoes covering my feet with peace. I was solid in my beliefs, and so, I started praying.

Oddly enough, it was not what I would have expected to have prayed in an emergency. Rather than asking for solutions or making promises I knew I couldn't keep in exchange for Anthony's miraculous healing, I assumed everything had already been worked out and that the call for the ambulance was precautionary, not life-saving. I thanked God for being with my son that day. I thanked Him for positioning my husband to be at home early from work that day. I declared that this day was special. Normally, Anthony mowed the lawn before his dad or I came home from work. Had the accident happened with him being alone at home, this could have turned out very differently. Yet, I believed even then that God had something awesome hiding behind whatever tragedy I was headed toward. Dre was with him. God was with them both. I prayed for his hands—that they would not be affected by this accident. "Father, my son loves working with his hands, and You have given him the gift to work on cars and machines... Please don't let this be his hands," I pleaded. With that plea, I glanced down at my phone and saw the next message.

"Meet us at LeBonheur. The ambulance is here, and we are going to the emergency room. He ran over his foot with the lawnmower."

"Praise God!" I said out loud. Prayer answered!

This was only the beginning of that day's prayers. As I exited the freeway and turned the car around to head back to the children's hospital, every second of every minute was filled with prayer and praise. Prayer and praise—those two things served as my foundation for keeping me calm over the next few hours. I imagined Anthony healthy and performing better on the court than ever before. I imagined him tinkering with cars and other electronic gadgets. I specifically and intentionally forced myself to stay positive, even during the few moments I wanted to fall apart. Of course, I arrived at the hospital sooner than my husband and son. There in the ER waiting area, I sat between the check-in station and the front sliding glass doors, oblivious to anyone else in the room at that moment. I distinctly recall other people were present, but I felt like I was the only person in that waiting area. When the ambulance arrived roughly ten minutes later, a nurse escorted me to the back door, and there my husband stood waiting to embrace me, shielding me from actually looking in my son's direction.

Can you even imagine that? Here I was waiting to see my son and his foot, and everyone was blocking my view, restraining me from getting in close proximity to him. Then I heard, "Mom! Mom! I'm okay. I'm okay." Anthony was yelling so I could hear him, but it really sounded like my baby was in a drunken stupor. When I think of a young man coming home from a drunken night out partying with his friends, I imagine that voice. His words were slurred; his eyes were wide open. I could see him smiling through tears, both wet and dry, on his face.

"I'm okay! I'm fine! I'm okay!" he kept reassuring me repeatedly until I relented to standing back and outside of the medical team's way. While it may have been prayers and praise that helped me manage that moment, I am certain the amount of morphine pumping through my son's veins offered its own powerful kind of relief all its own. As the countless doctors, nurses, paramedics, and other medical staff worked on Anthony, my husband told me the story.

Apparently, my husband had come home early from work that day and saw that Anthony hadn't mowed the lawn yet. Even though the grass was still a little damp from rain a few nights prior, Dre brought the unkept lawn to his attention. Grudgingly, Anthony had gotten out the mower and started mowing the backyard. The lawn in the back dips downward toward the fence line. Anthony was mowing along the fence and stood at the highest level while pushing the power down and forward. As he pulled the mower back, his foot slipped and went underneath the mower. The engine turned off, and he figured he had cut his foot. So, he walked back into the house and told Dre. Dre took off his shoe, and before he could even get his sock pulled off, he could see the damage was more than either of them realized. That's when he called the ambulance and texted me. Standing there between the nurse's station and the team working on my son, I knew my husband was hurting. He blamed himself for the accident, and all I could think of was how grateful I was that Dre was home when it happened. Anthony mowed the grass countless times without either of us being home. How could we have anticipated something like this? What if Dre hadn't come home early and Anthony had ended up mowing the lawn that day while alone? There was no way to know this would happen. Without even knowing the events that were to have transpired that day, God was with us.

Anthony was taken into surgery immediately. Dre and I sat in silence, not speaking a single word for hours. The hum of machines, the shuffle of nurses' shoes, the ticking of the wall clock—it was all background noise to the thoughts racing through my mind. I prayed. I imagined. I feared. But mostly, I waited.

When the surgeon finally emerged, I couldn't read his face. His expression was steady — practiced—the kind that could hold hope or heartbreak. "The damage is... significant," he began. "Anthony severed his second toe down to the first knuckle. The tip of his third toe is gone. And his big toe—"

He paused.

"It was sliced clean in half. Straight down the middle."

With one slip of the blade, the bone that bears weight and propels every forward step had been shattered. Not cracked. Shattered — into a million irretrievable pieces.

The surgical team had attempted to rebuild the toe from fragments, fusing what remained of the bone and cartilage with the hope that, over time, it would calcify — forming a new structure strong enough to support his walk.

"But we won't know for a while," the surgeon said gently. "If the fusion fails... We'll have to remove the toe."

He then said something to my husband, while I continued hearing *we'll have to remove the toe.* From that moment, everything else went dark. I don't recall anything between hearing those words and waking up the next morning on the couch in Anthony's hospital room, just as the nurse came in to check his blood pressure. He stayed in bed with his foot elevated and wrapped like a burrito for the next two days. We talked about him staying home for a few weeks while his foot recovered. I called his school to get his assignments and notify his teachers. Overall, he was in great spirits. He has always had a positive spirit about him. I love that about him.

On day three, the doctor insisted he get out of bed. Although he couldn't put any weight on his foot, they simply wanted him to get up and move around a bit. Get used to a wheelchair and crutches in preparation for his return home and school.

On a beautiful sunny day, four days later, we left room 212 and brought Anthony home.

The surgery was behind us, and a new routine had begun—one filled with gauze and antiseptic, weekly foot photos, quiet drives to the surgeon's office three times a week, and eventually, physical therapy.

Every day, a question hovered in the background:

Will he walk again?

The Healing

It was difficult to get out of bed the next morning, knowing that mornings were never going to be the same in our household. Anthony wasn't going to be running downstairs, sometimes missing a step (or three) to get to the first floor and out the door for school. It felt like everything we knew about living just one week prior was lost forever. Gone. There was a quietness in the house that was stiffening. The morning routine we had practiced since preschool—sleepy hellos, breakfast together in front of cartoons, laughing, talking homework, classes, or practices and games after school—they were all gone. A moot point.

It didn't take me but one of those silent mornings to know that we were going to need a new routine. Fast. With both Dre and me working, I needed to create a routine for Anthony that would have the greatest impact on not just his physical healing, but also on his emotional and mental healing. After all, how does a kid who lives and breathes basketball deal with the realization that he may never walk without a limp again? How does a kid like that process the possibility of not being able to run normally or do a backflip as his surgeon told him? Even walking into his room, there were reminders in every corner of his glory days (which were just last week) on the court, from the smallest of trophies to the King Kong-sized trophies from past championships. He was going to need more than his weekly visits to physical therapy and a new routine to get him to a new normal.

Determined to address my son's needs, our living room became Ground Zero for learning everything I could about his recuperation process. I relied on the surgeon and his team of physical therapists to normalize his foot again, but I had to take the lead when it came to healing his heart and his mind. Books, podcasts, songs, prayers, blogs, medical reports, scholarly journal articles, magazine articles, personal interviews with pastors, doctors, nurses, therapists, nutritionists, motivational speakers, YouTubers, and counselors. I left no resource untapped over the next three months. Eventually, five specific daily activities emerged as our routine. If I were Anthony's coach, these five things would provide the first five essential strategies for his playbook.

First, I had to tap into the same power of prayer I had used on the day of the accident. Those prayers helped me remain calm and provided me with the signs and evidence I needed to stay hopeful in that moment of chaos and uncertainty. Until that day, I would not identify as someone who was consistent in prayer, but I was now highly motivated, and consistency became relevant to his healing, and to be quite honest, to my own sanity. Prayer was, and now remains, my foundational daily habit.

Secondly, I needed to know more about Anthony's recovery possibilities. I needed to find time to research bone health, supplements, and nutrition for healing, careers in basketball other than courtside, resources for teen depression, and countless other topics. With a new job, there was no time during the day or night (if it was a game night) to conduct my own research. I had to find time to gain new information. Hence, setting aside small blocks of time to investigate important topics became crucial for our healing process.

Next, just as I had visualized a healthy son while waiting in the ER, I wanted to continue using visualization to create a new vision for our family, particularly for Anthony. I knew of many athletes who used visualization techniques to help them win championships or go to the Olympics. I had been creating vision boards for myself for years and knew about the Law of Attraction. Visualization was something I knew to be useful, and it was a technique I could teach Anthony so he, too, could start seeing new possibilities. Visualization could be done in a few minutes, could be depicted in a photo, and it could be used in conversation, so it was easy enough to incorporate regularly.

Next, I had to do a mental inventory of what was taking my focus away from my family. Having just started my dream job, I could not necessarily minimize my work, but I had to evaluate where I was spending my time, what sorts of things I had placed in front of my time with God in prayer or study, and where I was making myself the priority when I was needed elsewhere. I began to ask myself, what's the one thing I need to lay aside so that I can continue my focus on Anthony's recovery? A sacrifice now seemed easy since Anthony had just sacrificed his physical self, his dreams, and his self-confidence. I knew that some people fasted when they wanted to be closer to God, when they needed an answer, when they wanted to hear, but, for me, there were other things that I needed to get rid of, turn away from, or stop doing that were self-sacrificing. If I could give those things up to help me focus on God's direction for me, Anthony, and Dre, perhaps that would be more impactful. And so, exploring the one thing every day that I needed to let go of—that's where I placed my effort.

Finally, because I needed to focus as much every day as possible, I needed to manage my own health. How was I going to expect Anthony to invest time in getting stronger again if I did not stay healthy myself? Incorporating some form of exercise or using a focused diet at this time was crucial to my routine. Hence, training my body and my mind became a daily focus for us.

Rather quickly, these five things became part of my morning routine. Each morning, I woke up, went to the living room couch, opened a notebook, and started writing each day's version of the steps mentioned above in that notebook. I promised myself no less than five minutes in each area of focus. Five minutes of prayer and Scripture study. Five minutes of a Google search or time with YouTube for learning. Five minutes of visualization through meditation, phone apps, or podcasts. Five minutes of journaling about what I would let go of that day. Five minutes of working out, either riding on my Peloton, practicing yoga moves, or simply walking outside. And, what started out as a 25-minute morning routine organically turned into 60 minutes in the morning that I could not live without.

One day, my prayer would be short and succinct, while my time of learning about some trend in aromatherapy oils took 45 minutes. On another day, I would spend five to ten minutes in each area leading up to the last, and I would go for a three-mile walk as the last part of my morning routine. Over time, these action items became significant to my own mental attitude about the accident. Some 90 days later, I experienced significant changes:

- I lost 34 pounds by April 2019.

- I felt peaceful being at home.

- My blood pressure decreased.

- My skin looked better than it had in years.

- I found renewed optimism about Anthony's future, as well as for our family.

- I discovered a new ministry and calling for myself directly related to this new routine.

- And work did not weigh on me as much as it had in the first six months. The pace was still crazy hectic, but I felt calmer and more capable.

More important than what this routine did for me, though, is that this routine did for Anthony. Like, it REALLY worked.

- When my son returned to school just before Thanksgiving that year, and I saw how his friends rallied around him, helping him from one building to the next, carrying his books, and giving him rides, I knew my prayers were being answered. He had friends who truly cared about him and were willing to help. Another prayer answered!

- There was no limp after the bandages and the boot were removed and Anthony completed rehab. Answered prayer!

- When he came to me in early December and asked if he could play in a local basketball league with his friends, and I saw his hopefulness and his optimism, I knew the visualization work we had done was working. He had his confidence back. He felt healthy and happy. Answered prayer!

- He was able to run up and down the court again that January, playing with his friends on a weekend league (yes, I cried). The research done on nutrition, strength-building exercises, homeopathy, meditation, visualization, and countless hours of prayer ALL contributed to that moment. Answered prayer!

- Even today, Anthony eats healthy, drinks only water, and has maintained a healthy approach to cooking along with his own personal habits.

This approach to finding a new routine I had created for myself and for Anthony worked! Five years later, I still use these five things in my daily routine. I've coached others on the routine, and I have seen how its application in the workplace is equally effective. Now, I want to gift it to you.

Why it's called a PIVOT

The really interesting thing about Anthony's accident is which foot slipped underneath those blades. It was his right foot, specifically, the toe box. The toe box is what basketball players use to pivot when receiving the ball and planning a change in direction. The pivot foot stays grounded to the surface of the court while turning into a new direction. It remains grounded until the player has a visual on where he or she wants to take the ball, and when that destination is in sight, the pivot foot springs the player forward, moving them into a new direction.

Definition: PIVOT *(pi-vet)*

Used as a noun, a pivot is the pin or the central point on which something balances or turns; or, in a situation, it's the most important thing on which everything else is based or arranged around.

Remember the ingredients from the introduction on a good pivot?

7 Pivot Principles

- A pivot requires one to act. It requires decisions, right or wrong.

- A pivot requires a solid foundation.

- The triple threat position assumes the player is prepared for multiple outcomes. Pass, dribble, or shoot. Preparation is key.

- A pivot requires intentional movement, forward or reverse, depending on the circumstances being experienced at the time of the pivot.

- A player is either protecting the ball, creating space for other plays, prepping to be passed, or prepping to be shot, while moving within the pivot.

- A successful pivot will require recalibration to maintain balance.

- Finally, players who pivot well train their bodies and mind to be able to use either foot as the pivot foot. They intentionally train opposite muscle groups to be able to perform the same act.

I now call our transformational routine, The PIVOT Routine.

Here are the five truths of an effective PIVOT Routine:

1. **Pray** – This is your solid foundation.

2. **Inquiry** – This is your practice time.

3. **Visualize** – This is your anticipation of completing the pivot.

4. **Offering One Thing** – This is the sacrifice needed to become the best 'player' you can be.

5. **Train** – This is your body, mind, and soul transformation.

Now that you have the original pivot story, and you have the five keys to a successful daily pivot...

What kind of pivot are you facing?

Like our pivot, you may not even see a change forthcoming, but rest assured, just as I said in the first line of this book: change happens. Are you ready to deal with it?

How will you handle it when your company decides whether your position can be outsourced or is no longer needed? Mergers happen when their employees least expect them, and no matter how much they say the effects will be minimal, they somehow always involve employee turnover.

Are you looking for purpose in your life? Maybe you haven't figured out what 'your thing is' that you want to pursue every day. (That's okay, by the way. You figure it out along the way.)

Like my family, have you already experienced some sort of unexpected change, and are still trying to figure out how to find your new normal?

The PIVOT Routine was created for you to help you navigate that change that's in front of you. Change can be scary, exciting, even confusing.

But I am convinced that with a good PIVOT each day, you can tackle anything.

You can change jobs... without having a Plan B. (I certainly did!)

You can navigate difficult relationships.

You can go out on your own after a break-up.

You can recover and find purpose in a devastating medical diagnosis.

You can find, or even rediscover, your passion.

You can become your best self.

And you can heal your wounds, even the kind that happens unexpectedly.

Over the next few chapters, I will walk you through how to create your own PIVOT Routine. You may or may not be a religious or spiritual person, but the foundation of the pivot will help you identify and strengthen what's already in your heart, whether it's prayer and a relationship with God or establishing a purpose and passion to drive you through life. At the beginning of each chapter, you'll also see a Doctor's Note on Anthony's post-accident healing. I believe this will give you a physician's insight into both Anthony's physical healing and the transformation he underwent as these important principles started being applied to his own change in direction.

I'm going to coach you to learn techniques for maximizing your time throughout the day, how to set and manage your goals, and how to identify what's blocking your blessings. I will give you the basketball-mom perspective on visualization techniques used by coaches and athletes across different sports. With stories, anecdotes, and an Athlete's Spotlight to go with each PIVOT principle, you'll know more about Kobe Bryant, LeBron James, Michael Phelps, and other great athletes than you ever thought you would want to know.

At the end of each chapter, you'll also get Practice Drills you can incorporate into your PIVOT habit practice every day. Choose one to start until you're ready to try another drill. Athletes use drills for a variety of reasons, but muscle memory is the one we're going to lean into as you begin your PIVOT routine. If you're exploring how to visualize your transformation, your new job, your new life after a break-up, your new body after weight loss (or gain), the practice drills are what you must include every day to get your body and mind to remember the changes you are adopting. Practice drills are also used to simulate real-life scenarios, helping you develop your decision-making skills, so I'll give you space in each chapter to write your thoughts, take notes, and answer coaching questions.

Together, we are going to work on building your focus on positive and purposeful thoughts, building your resilience and confidence so you can tackle any circumstance that comes your way in life. Whether you are a 20-year-old athlete with a torn meniscus facing surgery, a 32-year-old who has just been fired, or a 50-something-year-old who is facing divorce, the PIVOT routine will provide you with your very own playbook to discover hope, a sense of stability you can depend on, and real joy in this uncertain and ever-changing world.

2

P STANDS FOR PRAYER
(OR PURPOSE)

Post Op Doctor's Note:

9/28/2018 – Anthony is a 16-year-old young man who injured his right foot on 09/25/2018. He caught the big toe and 2nd toe in a lawnmower. Had surgery at LB. Partial amputation. His proximal phalanx and distal phalanx were fixed with K-wires. Extensor tendon was reattached. Pain is moderate. As of today, he has five pins in place. The great toe looks like the wounds are intact and clean. The tissue looks viable.

"YOU HAVE TO BE ABLE TO CENTER YOURSELF, TO LET ALL OF YOUR EMOTIONS GO. DON'T FORGET THAT YOU PLAY WITH YOUR SOUL AS WELL AS YOUR BODY."
—KAREEM ABDUL-JABBAR

Over the next few chapters, you will understand the what, why, where, and how of all things PIVOT. As you finish each chapter, your responsibility will be to tailor the information I've provided to fit your needs. We all have different perspectives, different lenses through which we see life, and that's perfectly okay. Our differences are what make us so good together! So, whether you are looking at using the PIVOT Routine for work, for your relationships, to prepare for entrepreneurship, to find more peace in your daily hustle, or you're simply seeking to discover a better you, anyone can use this daily routine. Remember—this routine will give you as much as you put into it.

Let's begin with the foundation: prayer.

If you are reading this and do not have a current prayer practice or don't consider yourself a person of faith, that's okay—this routine is still for you. You can think of prayer as a moment of quiet intention, reflection, or grounding. Instead of prayer, you might use this time to journal your thoughts, meditate, express gratitude, or simply breathe and set your focus for the day. The goal is the same: to start your morning centered, clear, and connected to what matters most to you. If it's not prayer, it's all about your purpose. Whether it's prayer, reflection, or stillness, what's most important is that you start with purpose.

Let's go.

Just like in basketball, a strong pivot routine starts with a firm foundation. So, before we go any further, I need you to pause, grab a pen, and be honest with yourself. This is about you—your core, your stability, your center. These questions aren't just for reflection; they're here to help you name your foundation, so you know what you're standing on when life gets shaky.

Think back to your upbringing or defining seasons—who or what shaped your core values? How do those values influence the way you show up today?

____

____

____

____

____

List 3–5 values that guide your decision-making (e.g., integrity, empathy, growth). Then reflect: when was the last time one of those values was tested? How did you respond?

____

____

____

____

What's one daily rhythm, spiritual practice, or relationship that helps you feel grounded during uncertainty? Describe what it does for your mindset.

____

____

____

____

____

Imagine your life as a house. What core beliefs or habits make up the foundation, walls, and roof? Which areas feel strong—and which might need reinforcing?

____

____

____

____

____

We all know that a 'foundation' is simply a base on which something rests. Every well-built home stands firm because of what's beneath it. Without that foundation, the home crumbles. The same goes for you.

And every good pivot on the court—whether that's basketball, tennis, or pickleball—requires a solid base. A player must be planted before they pivot. Without that, they risk turning an ankle, losing control, or falling flat. It's no different in life.

Your foundation, whatever it is, should provide you with stability. It should be something you can return to—something that centers you and reminds you of who you are and why you're here. It should be steady. Unshakeable. Enduring. Something that doesn't collapse under stress or shift with every opinion or trend.

And here's the truth: **if your beliefs and values are shaped only by people or external circumstances,** you might be standing on shaky ground. People change. People leave. They make mistakes. They burn out. They pass on. You can love people deeply without building your identity on them.

The foundation of your life must be **bigger than the people in it.** It must be something that will still be standing when everything else falls away.

For some, that foundation is God—a personal relationship with a Creator who is constant and trustworthy. For others, it's a clear sense of purpose, a mission, or a core set of truths that guide their steps and ground their mindset.

Whether you start your day in prayer, meditation, journaling, or stillness, the key is this: start your day rooted in something that holds you up when everything else is trying to pull you down.

Because here's the real challenge: **if you don't choose your foundation, life, or family, or the government, or society, or something, will choose one for you.** And chances are, it won't be strong enough to carry the weight of your calling when the pressure comes.

Let's keep reading.

Prayer is the first element of a good PIVOT because it is the mechanism for discovering your foundation. Prayer will be the ground floor upon which you build the rest of your day, every day, as you embrace this new routine. Using prayer as the foundation for the rest of your day, you will experience six key outcomes over time:

1. Connection with God

    Whether you are a believer in God or not, prayer opens you up to building a personal relationship with our Creator. Prayer is a way to communicate, share thoughts, and seek guidance, and, if you are reading this book, I suspect that guidance is something you are in need of, right?

2. Alignment with God's Will

Have you ever ridden in a car that is out of alignment? It's a pretty bumpy ride. You're driving straight, but the car keeps pulling to the left or the right, and you are constantly having to make adjustments just to continue moving forward. It's the same in life. If you are out of alignment with God's will for your life, you will not experience true peace. You will not be able to rest knowing your decisions are sound. You will not be able to move forward in a straight line because you will get pulled left, right, or even backward. Incorporating prayer into your daily routine allows you to seek His guidance and wisdom, helping you to make decisions in line with your purpose (Reece, 2024). Prayer keeps you aligned with a great vision for your life.

3. Strength and Hope

Prayer provides strength and hope, especially during challenging seasons. Daily connection to the One who created the entire universe reminds us that we are not alone, even in times when we feel we are alone. Your daily prayer will, with consistency, give you the strength you need to move forward, to apply for that dream job, to resolve the relationship problem you are having, to apply for the small business loan, to ask for forgiveness from that friend or colleague, or whatever else you want to accomplish.

4. Humility and Compassion

   While you may not be looking for a little humility, regular prayer can foster humility and compassion. Our lives are not simply about us. It's not just about you. Did you know that there are millions of people around the globe praying for what you have? A regular routine of prayer will remind you that life is not only about you, but it's also about serving and helping others.

5. Peace and Comfort

   Just as I felt peace back in September 2018 while driving to the emergency room to meet my son and husband, unsure of what happened, you will find peace and comfort when you incorporate prayer into your daily routine. I can never truly put into words how I felt that day, but peace and comfort were with me. I did not have to worry about the outcome because I knew I could trust in God's plan for my son. I knew He would course-correct and realign Anthony on a path that would benefit him more than the path we already had in place for him.

6. Wisdom and Guidance

   When you're navigating life, isn't it good to have some wisdom available as your resource? How about a guide? Prayer provides those moments alone with God when you will begin to hear God's voice. You will feel His nudging you toward or away from something. Prayer will open up a dialogue with God and allow you to receive the direction you seek.

As the foundation for your five new daily habits, prayer will support not only your spiritual growth, but it will also serve as the base for your emotional health and a deep connection with God. Get ready, because you are about to grow in so many ways!

When, Where, and How to Pray

Any time is the best time to pray. But for the purpose of starting your new PIVOT routine, I encourage you to begin your day with just five minutes of intentional connection. For some, that's prayer. For others, it may be quiet reflection, journaling, or simply sitting still long enough to listen to your own thoughts. Whatever form it takes, the power is in the pause.

You can pray or reflect while lying in bed before the day begins. You can kneel beside the bed. You can curl up in your favorite chair, sit on your porch, or find a spot that feels like your own sacred space—even if it's just a corner of your kitchen table. There's no wrong place to pray or pause. But I do want to encourage you to make it your first priority. There is something deeply grounding about starting your day with intention. It anchors you. It softens your spirit. And it places the most important relationship—or the clearest sense of your purpose—front and center.

For me, it's journaling. Most mornings, I wake up, let the dogs out, grab a glass of water, and sit on the couch with my pen and notebook. That's where I talk to God. Sometimes I pray silently. Sometimes I speak aloud. But most of the time, I write. And when I write, I can be specific. I can be honest. I can write hard things—things that I don't want to give a voice to. But through journaling, I can give voice to my praise, my emotions, my fears, my doubts, and my long list of dreams and worries. I ask hard questions. I express gratitude. I write down the names of people I love or those who are struggling. Sometimes, I don't even know what to say—but I show up anyway.

And, friend, you don't have to be perfect with your words. You just have to be present. If you're new to prayer—or if you're still figuring out what you believe—this time can still hold power. Use it to ask deeper questions. Use it to reflect. Use it to speak life over yourself. Whether you're connecting with God, setting your intentions, or simply breathing through a moment of silence, what matters most is that you show up with honesty and openness.

You don't need the right words. You just need a willing heart.

I remember one morning after my son's surgery, when my heart was heavy and my words felt stuck. I couldn't form a polished sentence, much less a prayer. I just sat on the floor with my journal in my lap, tears falling on the page. I didn't say anything profound. I didn't even write that much. But in that moment, the silence felt sacred. It was like God met me right there—in my exhaustion, in my surrender. That five-minute pause didn't fix everything. But it reminded me I wasn't alone. And that reminder gave me the strength to keep going.

Whether your five minutes are filled with Scripture, silent reflection, or scribbled thoughts in a notebook, I want you to begin your PIVOT there.

You don't have to get it right. You just have to get started.

Putting Prayer into Practice

Now that you've learned the first step in your daily PIVOT routine—prayer—it's time to bring it off the page and into your life. And there's no better time than today. Not next Monday. Not after the holidays. Today.

Because just like a basketball player who's just been handed a new play, you don't wait until the championship game to try it out—you start small. You practice it. You fumble through it. You run the drill a few times and figure it out as you go. That's how mastery begins: not in perfection, but in motion.

So today, I want you to find just **five minutes.** Five minutes of stillness. Five minutes of conversation with God—or reflection, if you're still figuring out what prayer looks like for you. It could be a whispered thought, a written journal entry, or a moment of quiet while you're walking outside. Don't overthink it. This moment is yours.

Here are a few ways to make your practice more intentional and meaningful:

1. Start with Journaling

    Writing out your prayers or thoughts can be especially powerful. It keeps your focus and helps you go deeper than a quick mental note to God or the universe.

    Pro Tip: Write the date at the top of your page. This creates a timeline of transformation.One day, you'll look back at the things you prayed for, hoped for, or wrestled with—and realize how many of them have shifted, healed, or been answered. It's one of the greatest gifts of spiritual or personal reflection: perspective.

2. Try Speaking Aloud

    If writing isn't your thing, try speaking your prayers aloud. You can do it in your car, in the shower, on a walk, or in the quiet of your room. The sound of your own voice speaking truth, gratitude, or petition can be incredibly grounding. It makes your intentions real. Tangible. Alive.

3. Breathe and Reflect

    Still not sure what to say? Just sit and breathe. Let your thoughts come and go. You don't have to fix anything or come up with the perfect words. Just breathe deeply, and let this be your offering:
    - "Thank You for today."
    - "Show me where to grow."
    - "I don't know what to say, but I'm here."

    God hears even your silence.

4. Create a Sacred Space

    Over time, designate a spot in your home—however small—where you go for your five minutes. Light a candle. Grab your favorite pen. Set your phone to Do Not Disturb. Having a consistent environment helps signal to your heart that it's time to go inward and connect.

5.   For Those Still Exploring Faith

If you're still unsure about prayer, that's okay. You can use this time to:

- Set your intentions for the day
- Reflect on a powerful quote or piece of wisdom
- Practice a moment of gratitude
- Ask yourself: What matters most to me right now? What am I learning?

Think of this as a "mental reset"—a quiet moment of clarity that grounds your spirit before the world pulls at your energy.

Prayer doesn't have to be fancy or formal. It's simply the practice of turning inward, lifting your eyes to something greater, and anchoring your day with purpose. Some days, your five minutes will feel transformational. Other days, it may feel flat. Keep showing up anyway.

Because something powerful happens when you consistently make space for what matters most.

Let today be your first step. Your first rep. Your first pivot.

Let's go.

ATHLETE
Spotlight

🏈 Russell Wilson
Foundation Built on Faith

Russell Wilson, Super Bowl-winning NFL quarterback, is widely known not just for his precision on the field but for his unwavering commitment to faith and prayer. His success isn't accidental—it's deeply rooted in spiritual discipline and a daily routine centered around seeking God first.

Wilson often speaks about starting each day with scripture, prayer, and intentional alignment with God's will—especially in high-pressure environments like game day or leadership roles as a quarterback.

> "I've always been a believer that God has a bigger purpose
> for us than just winning football games.
> Faith is the foundation of everything I do—on the field and off it."
> — Russell Wilson

P – Prayer: Russell uses prayer as the literal starting point for every decision—whether it's leading a team, mentoring young athletes, or serving in the community.

Foundation: His consistency in faith during both career highs and lows (including injuries, team changes, and public scrutiny) shows what it means to build on something unshakable.

Public Witness: He isn't shy about giving glory to God in interviews, speeches, and his nonprofit work, modeling what it looks like to lead with humility and spiritual conviction.

Prayer Prompts

What do you hope to gain from adopting a new daily routine?

____

____

____

____

If you could ask God to help you with one thing today, what would that be? Why is this important to you?

____

____

____

____

What are you thankful for?

____

____

____

____

Practice Drills: Other Ways to Get Your 5 Minutes of Prayer

- Use an app on your phone. There are tons of available apps that can provide a verse-of-the-day, daily prayers, devotionals, motivational scriptures, and more. I use the Bible app. It's free, allows me to see what my friends are reading, and provides micro-video devotionals.

- Find a devotional book or app and commit to reading it first thing in the morning to get your day started.

- Instead of turning on the music in your car right away, take the first few minutes to talk to God while you're driving.

- Prayer walks. As you're exercising, particularly if you're a walker or runner, hold a conversational prayer.

- Start a gratitude journal. Each morning or every night before going to bed, list 3-5 things you are thankful for, and simply thank God.

- Keep it simple with personal requests. Say them, meditate on them, and then be quiet.
  - "Examine me, Lord."
  - "Forgive me, Lord."
  - "Fill me with Your Spirit, Lord."
  - "Restore me and strengthen me, Lord."
  - "Grant me wisdom, Lord."
  - "Protect my mind, Lord."
  - "Protect me, Lord."
  - "Help my unbelief, Lord."
  - "Guard my behavior, Lord."
  - "Arrange significant divine appointments, Lord."
  - "Enlarge my sphere of influence, Lord."

3

I STANDS FOR INQUIRY

Post-Op Doctor's Note:

10/3/2018 – Anthony returns. Did a dressing change today. His wound is healing and granulating. There is some macerated tissue, but no signs of deep infection. We ordered a home health nurse for dressing changes every 2-3 days at home. I will see him back in a week to reassess. The sutures will remain in place for about 6 weeks.

"OBSTACLES DON'T HAVE TO STOP YOU. IF YOU RUN INTO A
WALL, DON'T TURN AROUND AND GIVE UP.
FIGURE OUT HOW TO CLIMB IT."
—MICHAEL JORDAN

Now that you've committed to spending five minutes a day in prayer, centering your heart and aligning your intentions, let's move to the next essential part of a good PIVOT: inquiry.

This is where things start to shift.

Because let's be honest: if you're praying for a breakthrough, a transformation, or even just a little more peace—but you're not willing to move, to learn, to act—then you're not partnering with the change. You're just passively waiting for it to find you.

That's not how pivots work.

Picture this: a basketball player on the court catches the ball and plants their foot. What happens next? They pivot. They scan the court. They assess the defense. They look for an opening. But they don't just stand there holding the ball. They get curious. They move. They investigate.

Your daily inquiry practice is just like that.

If you want something in your life to shift—your career, your health, your relationships, your confidence— then you must become an active participant in the change you're expecting. Let me say that again: **YOU are an active participant in the change you are expecting.** This is your ball. Your moment. Your move.

The life you want isn't going to fall into your lap like a favor—it's waiting for you to step forward like a learner. Every day. With open eyes, a curious spirit, and a heart ready to grow.

And just like the best athletes in the world don't stop training once they make the team, you, too, must put in your daily reps of learning. Whether it's listening to a podcast on the way to work, picking up a new book, asking a better question, or Googling a topic that's been lingering in your mind—these small acts of inquiry become the building blocks of your transformation.

Research confirms what many of us have felt in our own lives: continuous learning is good for the brain and essential for the soul. It improves memory. It strengthens problem-solving. It boosts mental agility and keeps us engaged in the world around us. Lifelong learners are better equipped to handle change, process emotions, and adapt when things don't go as planned.

But it's not just cognitive—it's deeply personal.

Learning new things fuels confidence. It sparks creativity. It gives you momentum when you feel stuck. Whether you're mastering a new skill, exploring a forgotten passion, or simply broadening your worldview, every act of inquiry expands your potential.

And here's the best part: you don't need a classroom or a certification to start. You just need curiosity. A hunger to know. A willingness to ask:

"What don't I know yet?"
"What's next for me to discover?"

As someone who has worked in human resources for over fifteen years, I've seen it time and again—those who continue to learn rise faster, navigate challenges better, and adapt more easily. New doors open. New language forms. And the people who once felt stuck suddenly find themselves equipped for the very future they prayed for.

That's the power of investigation. That's the power of showing up each day ready to grow.

Let's pivot into it.

Finding a Steady Rhythm of Learning

Athletes don't become great by accident. Their growth is fueled by a steady rhythm of learning—on the court, off the court, and deep within their mindset. It's not just about strength or speed. It's about discipline, adaptability, and an unrelenting curiosity for what's possible.

Physical training, for example, is never random. Athletes engage in drills and repetition, practicing the same movements over and over until they become second nature. They review film—not just to relive victories, but to dissect mistakes, understand patterns, and sharpen their strategies. Many also embrace cross-training, stepping into different environments and trying new exercises to stretch their limits, stay sharp, and prevent burnout.

But their learning isn't just physical—it's deeply mental. Great athletes study the game like it's a language. They analyze plays, study their opponents' tendencies, and prepare mentally for every scenario. Visualization and mental rehearsal become tools to improve focus and execution, long before the lights of game day ever come on. And when setbacks happen? They don't waste the pain—they learn from it. They build resilience by asking, *"What can this teach me?"* instead of *"Why did this happen to me?"*

Coaching and feedback are integral to their growth. No one trains alone. Elite athletes seek one-on-one coaching to refine their technique, learn from teammates through observation, and review performance with mentors who hold them accountable to their highest potential. Every win, every loss, every moment becomes a lesson.

They also learn to listen—to their bodies and to the process. Recovery becomes as sacred as training. They adapt when things change, remain open to evolving methods, and stay grounded in the understanding that longevity requires care.

And perhaps the most powerful of all is their mindset. The greats are never done learning. They read books. They study psychology. They listen to interviews with other high performers. They reflect. They set goals. They challenge themselves constantly. Growth isn't an event—it's a habit.

Kobe Bryant embodied this with a level of curiosity that bordered on obsession. Yes, he was one of the most talented players to ever touch a basketball, but it wasn't just talent that made him great—it was his hunger to learn. He didn't just play the game. He studied it. He broke it down. He learned from retired legends like Michael Jordan and Hakeem Olajuwon, studied his opponents religiously, and read voraciously. He was multilingual, fluent in English, Italian, Spanish, French, and Serbian. He believed that the mind was just as important to train as the body—and his career reflected that belief.

Now, I'm not saying you need to speak five languages or break down films of your life like Kobe. But I am encouraging you to learn something new every day. Even if it's small. Even if it's inconvenient. Even if it takes five minutes between meetings or during your lunch break. Make learning a lifestyle. Make curiosity your coach.

I had to learn this lesson the hard way when Anthony got hurt. In those early weeks after his accident, I couldn't afford to sit still and hope things would improve. Every day became a search for answers. I found myself Googling everything from *recovery timelines for foot injuries* to *how long before a teen can walk after toe surgery.* I needed to know how to support him best, not just physically, but emotionally. Was there a natural remedy that would help with inflammation? Did we need to consider counseling? How soon was too soon to talk about his feelings, and what were the signs of depression in a high-performing teen who had just lost the game he loved?

My mornings began with articles on bone healing and orthopedic recovery. My evenings ended with forums of other parents who had walked a similar path. I dug into nutrition—figuring out how to support his body with the right foods. I looked into books for both of us, books that could help us mentally process the loss of normalcy and redefine what progress looked like. I learned how critical it was to let him rest—and how equally important it was to start gently encouraging movement. And when I wasn't sure if his mood was sadness or the early signs of depression, I asked. I reached out to a mental health expert and started looking into what kind of support he might need now—and in the months to come.

Like any dedicated athlete—or any determined mom—I studied. I researched. I showed up every day with curiosity and courage because I knew his healing would require more than doctor's visits. It would require leadership, learning, and love.

Because the more you learn, the more equipped you become—not just to change, but to thrive through that change.

What is something you've always wanted to learn but never had the time?

____

____

____

What is a topic or idea that excites you, even if you don't know much about it yet?

____

____

____

What's one thing you can explore today that will challenge you to think in a new way?

____

____

____

See? You've already thought of at least three topics you can explore to learn something today that you didn't know yesterday.

That season of life wasn't just about helping Anthony heal. It was about rebuilding what I thought I knew. It was about becoming the kind of woman who could lead through uncertainty—one question, one search bar, one article at a time. Every Google search was my attempt to be brave in the face of the unknown. It wasn't glamorous, but it was necessary. It was faith in action, disguised as curiosity.

And here's the truth: inquiry isn't just about information. It's about *empowerment.*

The more I learned, the more confident I became in asking the right questions at doctor visits. The more I read, the more I could advocate for Anthony's physical and emotional needs. I wasn't just supporting my son—I was retraining my brain to problem-solve from a place of clarity instead of chaos.

Some mornings, I didn't even know what I was searching for. I just knew I couldn't go back to bed without trying to learn something—anything—that could help me feel a little less powerless.

That's the real value of daily investigation. It builds resilience from the inside out. It reminds you that you are not stuck—you are still becoming.

So, whether you're Googling teen trauma recovery or listening to a podcast on leadership, whether you're reading a devotional or watching a TED Talk on healing— keep searching. Keep asking. Keep showing up for yourself and your future.

Because in the end, every new insight you gain is a small act of hope. And hope, my friend, is a powerful catalyst for change.

And yes—for a great PIVOT routine, you only need five minutes a day to start. That's how we did it. As Anthony slept during the early hours of the morning, I took out my laptop and Googled topics like *healing recipes for broken bones in teens* or *how to support my teen after surgery,* even *how to know if your teen is suicidal.* I searched everything from aromatherapy to muscle atrophy to local psychotherapists who specialized in teen trauma. I didn't wait for the answers to find me—I pursued them, one click at a time.

That's what daily inquiry looks like. It's not about being perfect. It's about being present.

And one last reminder: devoting just five minutes a day to learning something new will sharpen your focus, increase your emotional awareness, build critical thinking skills, and strengthen your ability to adapt in any environment. It will stretch you, mentally and emotionally, into someone who doesn't just survive change—but navigates it with wisdom, confidence, and grace.

That's the power of the daily pivot. So, start small. Stay curious. And keep learning your way forward.

ATHLETE
Spotlight

🏈 Dr. Myron Rolle
The Power of Curiosity in Every Arena

Dr. Myron Rolle is not your typical athlete.

A former NFL safety and Rhodes Scholar, Myron seamlessly combined elite athleticism with academic brilliance. After being drafted by the Tennessee Titans, he took a year off from football to study medical anthropology at Oxford University—then returned to the NFL. Today, he's a neurosurgeon at Harvard-affiliated Massachusetts General Hospital.

> "The same discipline I used to study film and prepare
> for football is the same discipline I use to study neurosurgery.
> Learning doesn't stop when the season ends—it evolves."
> — Dr. Myron Rolle

- Inquisitive Mindset: Myron approached both the gridiron and the classroom with deep curiosity. He saw learning not as a side goal, but as a central pillar of who he was becoming.

- Relentless Learning: From studying game strategy to mastering human anatomy, Myron embodies the idea that a successful life requires ongoing investigation, reflection, and adaptability.

- Purpose-Driven Growth: He used his learning journey to pivot from sports to medicine with a clear purpose—to serve others and save lives.

Inquiry Prompts

What is something you've noticed today that you've never really paid attention to before?

____

____

____

What's a question you keep circling back to in your quiet moments—about your future, your work, your relationships, or your growth? Why do you think it keeps coming up?

____

____

____

Who in your life do you admire for their sense of curiosity, and why?

____

____

____

What's one thing you can do today that will challenge you to think in a new way?

____

____

____

Practice Drills: Ways to Learn Something New Daily

- Listen to a podcast while multitasking, such as during a commute, workout, or household chores. Bonus points for taking notes.

- Listen to an audiobook during a commute or workout. Remember—it's just 5 minutes.

- Watch a documentary or educational video. There are great platforms to explore, such as YouTube, TED Talks, MasterClass, and others.

- Find a webinar or workshop of interest and register. Put it on your calendar and then show up.

- Participate in a group discussion. Engaging in conversations on platforms like online forums, social media groups, or study circles can expose you to diverse viewpoints and new ideas.

- Find a new recipe, purchase the ingredients, and cook.

- Find a smoothie recipe, purchase the ingredients, and drink.

- Learn a new hobby or sport. If you want to be an artist, do seven days of drawing faces, or learn to watercolor by watching YouTube videos.

- Find an online course and complete it. There are plenty of free and cheap ones out there on platforms like Udemy, Khan Academy, LinkedIn Learning, and Coursera.

- Download an interactive App on your phone. There's Duolingo for language learning or Skillshare for interactive learning. Find something interesting for you and follow-through.

- Find a coach or a mentor and start asking questions.

- Join Toastmasters International. Toastmasters International is a global organization that helps people become more confident communicators and leaders through regular, supportive practice in public speaking. It's a safe space to grow your voice, sharpen your message, and receive feedback that fuels real growth. There are local chapters everywhere! (This is a game-changer for real!)

- Attend a cultural event or travel to someplace new. This exposes you to new information through sensory experiences and interactions with different perspectives.

- If you speak in public, are an entrepreneur, or often find yourself needing to pitch a great idea, consider practicing on video. Like a great athlete, you can get so much from studying yourself on video.

4

V STANDS FOR VISUALIZATION

Post-Op Doctor's Note:

10/12/2018 – Anthony seems optimistic. He says his great toe looks viable. No signs of deep infection. His pins are still in place. The wounds are a little macerated. We redressed him today.

"IF YOU WANT TO BE THE BEST, YOU HAVE TO BE WILLING TO DO WHAT OTHERS AREN'T WILLING TO DO."
—ATTRIBUTED TO MICHAEL PHELPS

'll bet that at some point in your childhood, whether you were at school, on the playground, or even at home, you were told to use your imagination. Am I right? I am an only child, and imagination was essential to fight off everyday loneliness and boredom. In my mind, I had many friends who would often come over to the house and play with me for hours. Some had names, while others didn't.

Underneath the dining room table with Barbie, Ken, and Cher, I imagined my own world of grown-ups socializing together, sharing great meals, and camping in Barbie's camper. In my room, I was a teen rock star who could not only sing, but also dance and wear all the fashionable styles of the '80s. It was my imagination that allowed me to envision what it would be like to be all those things—a friend to many, a perfect girl like Barbie, or an American Idol, but my imagination stopped there.

Imagination, unlike visualization, allows us to create pictures or ideas in our mind. A healthy imagination can fuel our creativity, allow us to see possibilities beyond our realities, and even help us solve problems. So, how is imagination different from visualization?

Like our daily prayer and inquiry habits, visualization is intentional and action-oriented. Using one's imagination has no goal. The imagination is exactly what it is—mental images for the sake of experiencing and exploring. Like using our imagination, visualization is used to create mental images, but where they differ is this:

Visualization is used to create mental images of specific goals or outcomes.

Visualization is purposeful.

Wellness blogger, Kristine Moe, defines visualization best: "Visualization is the practice of imagining what you want to achieve in the future. As if it were true today." My goal was never to 'be' a rock star, or a fashionista, or someone who camps. My only goal as a little girl when using my imagination was to circumvent my boredom or loneliness. Our imagination sparks feelings, whereas visualization sparks results.

Let's read that again.

Imagination sparks *feelings.* Visualization sparks *results.*

I don't know about you, but when I think about my needs as an adult or a parent, results are what I need more in my life. I've learned over the years of watching basketball, and now being around the coaching staff and professional athletes of the NBA, that athletes provide a great example of using visualization to get results.

American swimmer Michael Phelps used visualization as his way of mentally rehearsing swim meets prior to competitions. His coach, Bob Bowman, believed "champions are forged in the mind before they dominate in reality." In preparation for competition, Coach Bob taught Phelps to use visualization to envision both positive outcomes and negative outcomes. Envisioning positive outcomes was essential to training, because as he swam, he felt as if he had already rehearsed. That pool was familiar. He knew the temperature of the water because he had already envisioned the temperature in his mind. He knew the depth of the pool because he had already envisioned it. He knew the length because, in his mind, he had already swum that race and won. Hence, his mental rehearsal gave him a sense of familiarity, and when you're in a competition, the familiarity of your path breeds confidence. Envisioning negative outcomes was essential, too, because preparing for everything that could happen during competition is imperative. What if his swimsuit became torn? What if a swimmer in the next lane accidentally swam into his lane? What if his foot flipped as he completed his flip turn? An athlete can only be prepared for these types of negative outcomes in one of two ways—by either experiencing them or visualizing them.

The Mental Power of Visualization

When you use visualization techniques, your brain doesn't just "imagine" success—it prepares for it. Visualization is more than wishful thinking. It activates your brain, strengthens emotional resilience, and fuels the motivation needed to step into something new, even when everything familiar has shifted.

Let's break down how it works and why it's such a vital part of the PIVOT Routine.

When you picture yourself doing something—whether it's delivering a keynote, landing a job, or starting a new chapter—your brain lights up as if you're actually doing it. That's right. Simply imagining an activity can activate the same motor cortex in your brain responsible for physical movement. This is why elite performers across disciplines— from athletes to CEOs—rely on mental rehearsal as a daily tool.

Take the world of sports. Mikaela Shiffrin, the Olympic skier, began her visualization practice at just three years old. Her parents would pretend their driveway was a ski slope, and Mikaela would mimic the movements of a skier. She wasn't just playing—she was preparing. Her brain was learning, wiring her for the future.

In my own house, we saw early rehearsals, too. At three, I was told I never stopped talking. Microphones weren't toys—they were part of my destiny. I was rehearsing for my future life as a speaker without even knowing it.

Simone Biles has openly shared how she mentally walks through every twist, tumble, and landing in her mind before she steps onto the mat. That rehearsal gives her confidence. Her mind has been there before—even when her body hasn't.

And then there's Serena Williams, who has spoken about the rush she feels during high-stakes matches. That rush is dopamine—the brain's motivation and pleasure chemical. Visualization can increase dopamine levels, giving you the same kind of motivational boost as physical activity. It's a neurological reward that drives performance, motivation, and even happiness.

I've seen this firsthand with my son Anthony. Before he found his rhythm in basketball, he tried other sports. Baseball held his attention for a few seasons—but not enough to spark real joy. Then came football. At just seven years old, he was already a quarterback and ran in two touchdowns in one game. But one big hit later, he was gasping for breath on the sidelines. The dopamine, as I like to say, got tackled right out of him.

Basketball, however, lit something different in him. It brought him joy, focus, and identity. So, when his injury pulled him away from the court, we had to find new ways to replicate that spark. We had to visualize a new future—one where he was still in the game, just in a different role.

And that's what visualization does—it helps you see yourself in a new place and start building mental connections toward it.

Visualization isn't about pretending everything goes perfectly. It's about preparing your mind for whatever may come. When you make it a consistent practice—not just in crisis but as part of your daily routine—you train yourself to pause, reset, and respond rather than react. That's the power of mental rehearsal: it strengthens your ability to pivot with intention instead of fear.

In the moments on the day of Anthony's accident, it could have been easy for fear to take over. And yes, I was tempted to go into my fear state, but without even knowing what I had done, I had trained for this moment using visualization in my own daily routine. This is why your visualization practice is so powerful. Creating an intentional visualization practice creates mental rehearsals that remind your brain how to respond with clarity, not chaos. You learn to regulate your emotions, quiet your fear, and anchor your thoughts.

When you're learning how to pivot—after a layoff, after loss, or even after a new diagnosis—visualizing a stronger, braver version of yourself can help you rewrite the story. Even if the circumstances are hard, your brain can rehearse success, wholeness, and healing. And that repetition builds real change.

Visualization also boosts your creativity. When Anthony couldn't play ball anymore, we asked a simple but powerful question: *What if the game doesn't stop—what if it just looks different?* We imagined new paths. Sports analytics. Team operations. Coaching. Performance psychology. There were more ways to be in the game than on the court. We just had to get creative. And visualizing those possibilities helped us stay hopeful and open to new directions.

Finally, visualizing success—consistently—reinforces the habits needed to get there. When you imagine yourself making healthy choices, delivering that powerful talk, or having the confidence to walk into your next opportunity, your brain gets familiar with that action. That familiarity breeds follow-through.

So, if you're in a season of transition, don't just wait for clarity to find you. Visualize it. Rehearse it. Activate it. Prepare your mind for the outcome you desire—and watch your heart begin to follow.

You've picked up this book for a reason. What change are you experiencing this season in your life? Write it down, acknowledge it, right now.

____

____

____

____

____

Remember the mental rehearsal Coach Bob taught Michael Phelps, the one where Phelps practiced visualizing both positive AND negative outcomes of a race? That wasn't just about winning medals. It was about *preparing for pressure.* The same strategy that helped him win gold can help you hold on to peace in uncertainty, confidence in the face of change, and joy even when the outcome isn't yet visible. When you practice seeing yourself in a new habit, a new mindset, or even a new role, you are forming your own mental rehearsal. You are training your mind to lead you where your body is not yet brave enough to go.

What new habit, new mindset, or new role are you looking at right now?

____

____

____

____

____

These neural rehearsals *matter*—because your brain doesn't distinguish much between imagined success and real success. That's why repetition matters. That's why the habit matters. Your brain is creating pathways that make the imagined more accessible and eventually, more possible.

Imagine right now if you were to embrace that new habit or new mindset. What if you actually got the job you were eyeing right now? What if you attracted the friends you longed for or the supportive co-workers you wanted? Write down what that looks like and how that makes you feel to have successfully achieved that habit, mindset, or goal.

____

____

____

Ever known someone who practically lives at the gym? I used to call them "gym rats" back in the day (and yes, I was one of them myself). But now I know better. Those people aren't just exercising—they're reinforcing a mental reward loop. Working out gives them energy, clarity, and results—and that positive reinforcement strengthens their commitment. The gym becomes less of a place and more of a *pattern*. And that's what visualization can do for you—it becomes the pre-game ritual that makes showing up easier. And all those mirrors you see at the gym? As much as it may seem to be a vanity prop, they are really just another visualization tool people use to reinforce their mental reward pattern.

Point guard and American professional basketball player with the Golden State Warriors, Stephen Curry, is another athlete who uses visualization, not just for performance but for peace. Before every game, he goes through the same quiet routine. He closes his eyes and mentally walks through his first three shots. He pictures the arc, the net, and the rhythm. He doesn't hope the shots will fall—he sees them falling before they leave his hands. It's no wonder he's one of the most accurate shooters in

NBA history. His body follows the vision his mind has already locked in.

But visualization isn't just for gold medalists or Most Valuable Players (MVPs). It's for you, too. Maybe you're visualizing yourself walking into the interview room with confidence. Or sitting across from a therapist and finally telling the truth. Or waking up at peace after months of waking up in fear. That vision is valid. That practice is powerful.

And it's biblical. In Habakkuk 2:2, God tells the prophet, "Write down the revelation and make it plain." Why? Because when we see the vision clearly, we begin to align our actions with it. Visualization is one way to do that. You're not just writing the vision—you're *rehearsing it into reality.*

So, whether your pivot is physical, emotional, spiritual, or professional, remember this: the brain responds to what you *repeat.* The more you visualize a habit, the more your brain makes room for it. And soon, what once felt unfamiliar becomes second nature. This is the heart of your PIVOT Routine. Not just moving forward blindly but stepping intentionally. Seeing it before you live it. Training your mind to lead your life. Because clarity doesn't always show up on command. It shows up where there is discipline, practice, and hope.

ATHLETE
Spotlight

Lindsay Vonn
Training the Mind to Win the Mountain

Lindsey Vonn, one of the most decorated alpine ski racers in history, is not only known for her physical strength and courage—but for her mental toughness and visualization habits that helped her dominate some of the most dangerous slopes in the world.

"Before I ever dropped into a race,
I had already skied it in my mind a hundred times.
Every turn, every jump, every possibility—I'd seen it.
So when it came time to race, I was just following the plan."
— Lindsey Vonn

- Purposeful Mental Rehearsal: Vonn famously studied video footage and then used vivid, repeated visualization to mentally ski each course before competition. She would sit quietly before every race, eyes closed, hands gripping imaginary poles, and ski the full course in her head—down to the milliseconds.

- Obstacle Planning: Her visualizations included both best-case scenarios and the unexpected—ice patches, bad landings, shifting conditions—so she was prepared for anything when she hit the slope.

- Mind-Body Alignment: Visualization helped her regulate fear, boost confidence, and align her mind and body to perform under pressure—especially after multiple injuries and surgeries.

Lindsey's ability to "see it before she skis it" made her one of the fiercest competitors on the circuit, and her mental preparation is widely cited as one of her greatest strengths.

Visualization Prompts

"See Her/See Him" Prompt

Close your eyes and picture the woman or man you're becoming.

1. What is she/he wearing? How does she/he walk into the room? What does her/his calendar look like? How does she/he respond under pressure?

   ____

   ____

   ____

2. Now, what small shift can you make today that brings you closer to her/him?

   ____

   ____

   ____

"Victory Moment" Prompt

3. Visualize the moment you achieve the goal you're working toward—whether it's a promotion, launching a business, crossing a stage, or finishing your book. Write it down here.

   ____

   ____

   ____

4. Where are you? Who's with you? What are you wearing? How do you feel in that moment?

   ____

   ____

   ____

Let that version of you anchor your why.

"Sacred Space" Prompt

5. Picture a peaceful place—real or imagined—where you can meet with God. Name this place right now.

    ____

6. What does it look like? What are you bringing to Him? What is He saying back to you?

    ____

    ____

    ____

This is your place of alignment. Return to it often.

"One Year From Now" Prompt

7. It's one year later, and you've stayed consistent with your PIVOT Routine.

    What does your life look like now—physically, mentally, spiritually, professionally?

    How do others describe you? How do you describe yourself?

    ____

    ____

    ____

    ____

    ____

"Next-Level Peace" Prompt

8. Imagine yourself walking through a chaotic moment with complete peace. What chaotic moment are you thinking of right now?

9. What are you doing differently? What are you not carrying anymore?

____

____

____

____

____

Let this mental movie become your blueprint for calm and confidence in real life.

Practice Drills: Incorporate Visualization into Everyday Moments

Choose one each day. Try several over an extended period of time to find out which ones work for you. Everyone is different. You may use one, several, or you may discover one that's not on my list.

- Vision boards – a collection of images and words that relate to an outcome. These can be done physically, using a poster board and magazine clippings, or you can use popular digital programs like Canva or phone apps.

- Visualization apps, like Happify, Headspace, EnVision, Vision Board 2024, Inkflow, and so many more.

- Guided meditation – Simply close your eyes and create those mental images in as much detail as possible. Imagine all the steps of a successful conclusion.

Then, go back to that same vision, adding more detail daily so that it becomes part of your daily routine.

- Word art – In my office, I have a large sign in the middle of a wall that reads, "Faith as small as a mustard seed can move mountains" (Matthew 17:20). That is the center of that wall with smaller art pieces framing those words. Every time I look at that wall, I recall the potential every mountain has in life, and I remind myself to believe in something bigger than myself.

- Pictures – Surround yourself at work or at home with specific photos or pictures of your goals. While it doesn't have to be an entire vision board, it can be simply one photo.

- Exposure – Expose yourself to elements of what you want to achieve until you're all-in and doing the thing you envisioned. For example, I have always wanted to hike the Grand Canyon. While I probably should have completed my Bucket List item when I was younger and fitter, I still have the dream to walk rim to rim. My exposure practice is to look up YouTube videos of women who have hiked the Grand Canyon in their 50s and older. What are their tips for success? I also search for different hiking companies, reviewing their customer reviews and interviewing their guides, to ask questions in preparation for my hike. I have also taken up a daily walking routine, and on weekends, I find hiking trails to complete in preparation for "the big hike."

- Index cards – Write 10 to 20 goals you have right now, each on its own index card, and review them each morning and night.
- Various journaling exercises
  - Balance Wheel exercise
  - Best Possible Self writing prompts
  - Write down what you want, using all your senses, and re-read daily
  - Create your own vision statement
  - Create your own mission statement
  - Create your values statement

5

O STANDS FOR OFFERING

Post-Op Doctor's Note:

10/17/2018 – Anthony returns today. It has been 3 weeks. He has had pins placed. Some home health care and dressing changes. Today, shows a viable toe. No signs of deep infections. Would have less maceration than previously. We removed some of his sutures today, a few we left in the great toe. Applied new dressing. We will see him back in about a week. Hopefully, we can get the remainder of the sutures out at that time. I do want him to continue dressing changes and continue to let the wound air out a bit between dressing changes. Dressing changes daily, sometimes twice each day.

"DON'T QUIT. SUFFER NOW AND LIVE
THE REST OF YOUR LIFE AS A CHAMPION."
—MUHAMMAD ALI

Let's just go ahead and say it—this might be the hardest part of your daily PIVOT. If you've made it this far, you've laid the foundation, gotten curious, and started visualizing a better version of your life. But here's the deal: none of that matters if you're not willing to give something up to get something greater.

In sports, athletes give up sleep, comfort, and sometimes even the scoreboard just to play the long game. In the faith world, it's about taking up your cross daily. And in everyday life, this is the moment you choose to release what's easy so you can reach what's next.

And no, I'm not talking about huge, dramatic sacrifices every single day. I'm talking about small, daily decisions that add up. Skipping the scroll so you can write the business plan. Saying no to the comfort food so you can feel better in your body. Letting go of the fear so you can finally hit send on that application.

It's not glamorous. It's not always fun. But if you want the life you keep saying you want, the job you want, the relationship you want, the family, the experience, the whatever—there will be something you have to offer up—comfort, control, convenience—something. Because nothing pivots if you stay exactly where you are.

This part? It's about learning to let go so you can move forward. One small sacrifice—your personal daily offering—at a time.

Most people aspire to greatness. A great wife. A great husband. A great mom. A great artist. A great professional. We all yearn to excel at something, yet few are truly willing to pay the price that greatness demands. Research in psychology shows that achieving long-term success often requires a high level of self-control and the ability to delay immediate rewards for future gains. This is often the point where dreams begin to fade for many—success doesn't happen overnight, and the path to greatness is paved with difficult choices and consistent effort. Anthony, for example, wanted to be a great basketball player—a dream that required more than just raw talent. In my twenties, I aspired to be a great fitness influencer, but the journey was far from easy.

Looking Back at Game Film

In my twenties, I had an amazing career with Lady Foot-locker as a Store Manager and Manager Trainer. I mean, AMAZING. Year after year, I earned awards for my sales and my ability to train new managers who went on to achieve success in their own stores. I won TVs, bicycles, trips, cruises to Puerto Rico, St. Thomas, and the Bahamas. I was recognized every quarter for three years in some top category for my team's sales. By the time I was 22 years old, I had a base salary of $40,000, which may not seem like much in 2025, but I did the calculation. That's more than $97,000 in 2025! I was a baller! I had everything I ever wanted, and I was only 22 years old. But you know what?

It wasn't enough.

I wanted more.

I had my eyes on a promotion. It wasn't enough to be a successful manager. I wanted to be a District Manager (DM) before I turned 25. But after realizing that the people above me loved their jobs just as much as I loved mine—and they were 30+ years from retirement—I saw that my path to becoming one of the youngest DMs in company history was blocked. If I wanted to make more money (which was a huge priority at the time), it wouldn't be as a Store Manager. I needed something more on my own terms.

So, with the encouragement of friends, I left my secure job, quit the benefits, quit the money, abandoned the dream, and decided to go all in. I taught aerobics five days a week and took a chance as a certified personal trainer, betting that within 6-9 months, I would be making as much, if not more, than I did at Lady Footlocker. I gave up alcohol. I gave up late nights socializing with friends. I gave up unhealthy but oh-so-delicious foods, and I even gave up dating (which, honestly, was probably for the best). I hired a dietitian and started journaling every morsel of food, every bicep curl, dip, and step taken at the gym. I took up hiking, white-water rafting, and mountain climbing as my new hobbies away from the gym. I was chasing my dream. And all of this, in the pursuit of a bigger goal—becoming a fitness competitor, trainer, and influencer.

Side-huddle: Let me pause here and keep it real with you.

There was a season when I chased the dream of becoming a professional fitness competitor. I earned my Pro Card—which is no small feat—but never made it to the stage. Truth? I was scared. Scared of being judged. Scared of not measuring up. And honestly? Tired. I also became a certified Personal Trainer through the International Sports Sciences Association (ISSA) and worked with clients for several years. I poured myself into my dream of becoming a ranked and titled competitor. I tracked macros. I trained hard. I did all the things!

But deep down, I was craving more than six-pack abs and protein shakes.

The reality? I wanted pizza again.

(It's okay, you can laugh.)

Even though I never made that dream come true, that season in my life taught me discipline, drive, and how to show up. More importantly, it also taught me when it's time to pivot. And I did.

So, if you've ever felt torn between the "highlight reel" version of success and what actually feeds your soul, I get it. This isn't about perfect routines. It's about *aligned* ones. Pivots are personal. And powerful. And sometimes, they include pizza.

Now—let's get back to yours.

...

We all know someone who's chasing a dream. This could be you, too. But here's the real question: **Are you prepared to sacrifice what's truly necessary to become that person you want to be?**

Greatness isn't handed to us; it's earned through daily commitment, hard choices, and the willingness to do what others won't.

Small Decisions, Big Wins

Eliud Kipchoge is widely regarded as the greatest marathon runner of all time, but his success is not merely a product of natural talent. It is the result of a lifetime of small, consistent sacrifices. Kipchoge made history on October 12, 2019, when he became the first human to complete a marathon in under two hours, finishing the 26.2-mile (42.2 km) race in 1:59:40 during the INEOS 1:59 Challenge in Vienna, Austria. While this achievement did not count as an official world record due to the controlled conditions—such as pacers, laser-guided pacing, and fluid handoffs—it shattered previous beliefs about the limits of human endurance. In addition to this legendary feat, Kipchoge holds the official marathon world record of 2:01:09, set at the Berlin Marathon in 2022. He is also a two-time Olympic gold medalist (2016, 2021) and has multiple victories in major marathons like London, Berlin, and Chicago.

In a world of excess, Kipchoge lives in simplicity. While the world's best athletes train in state-of-the-art facilities, he chooses to live in a spartan training camp in Kenya, sleeping in a tiny, shared room with no luxuries. He really reminds me of Rocky Balboa. Remember when he became the champ, but he got soft in his training? What did he do? He went to Russia in the heart of winter, stayed in a barn, chased chickens for speed, and walked in four feet of snow with a hundred-pound log on his neck. No luxuries. And Kipchoge, he could dine in five-star restaurants, but instead, he eats the same basic meal of ugali (that's cornmeal porridge) and vegetables every day. He could drive luxury cars, but he prefers to ride his bike. As for me, I'm no world marathoner or boxer, but I, too, knew that the sacrifices I made each day would eventually pay off. I ate a very limited assortment of chicken, rice, broccoli, eggs, and protein drinks. (Well, except for Fridays. Fridays were my day off from dieting. Lunch was usually Chinese food with friends from the gym, and dinners were always ham and pineapple pizza delivery while my roommates went out and I stayed in to watch TV.)

Why the extreme measures?

Because discipline is *freedom*.

Every morning before dawn, while most of the world is still asleep, Kipchoge is already running—logging hundreds of miles each month, no excuses, no distractions. He doesn't chase motivation; he chases mastery. And mastery requires sacrifice.

The moment Kipchoge shattered the world record for fastest marathon wasn't about two hours—it was about every decision he made when no one was watching. Every early morning run. Every meal choice. Every moment he said "no" to comfort and "yes" to discipline.

That's the reality of real change. It doesn't come from grand gestures or occasional bursts of inspiration. It comes from the daily, deliberate choices to be better. To push through the pain. To ignore the doubts. To sacrifice what is easy for what is necessary.

The question isn't whether you have the potential for greatness. You do.

The real question is: **Are you willing to pay the price?**

In your daily PIVOT, you need to be aware of what you are willing to do, to offer up, to sacrifice today to move towards the change you're trying to adopt. And don't get overwhelmed here. I'm not asking you to sell your house to go live in a yurt. I'm not asking you to give up family dinners or lunches with your girlfriends just so you can live on broccoli, rice, and baked chicken every day. Everyone has something they could give up in order to transform. You just need to do some critical thinking about what your one thing is for today.

Let's get some reps in now to help you think more deeply about your priorities, trade-offs, and long-term vision. These journaling prompts can help you reflect on what you are willing to sacrifice today to transform into who you want to be or what you want to accomplish tomorrow.

What does greatness look like for you in 20 years?

____

____

____

Why does achieving this matter to you on a deep level?

____

____

____

What's at stake if you don't commit to this journey? (Coach's Clue: What you do [or don't do] not only affects you, but it also affects people around you, people you will never meet, people who haven't even been born yet. The way you think about how you're NOT doing the work will affect the future.)

____

____

____

What are you currently doing that's holding you back from your goals?

____

____

____

What habits, distractions, or comforts are you willing to let go of today to move closer to your vision?

____

____

____

Side-huddle: This might be more than you bargained for when you purchased this book, but I need to interject a little truth about my own journey.

I struggle with vanity.

No, seriously. I'd say I'm a 5 out of 10 in the looks department, but what I lack in beauty, I make up for in boldness and personality. And yet, as someone who's on stage, inspiring others, trying to walk boldly in her purpose—it can be hard when your self-consciousness tries to show up with you.

My biggest insecurity? My hair. It's thin, fragile, and no longer what it used to be in my twenties. Back then, I had a lion's mane. I could perm it, dye it, tease it, and toss it. But years later, my hair can't keep up with my demands. I had to choose to either keep damaging it or surrender to caring for it.

So, in 2019, after my son's accident, after he returned to school and basketball, I made a decision. I would focus my PIVOT Routine on something that challenged me in a real, tangible way. I gave up all heat tools—no curling iron, no blow dryer—for 31 days. It was my No Heat January.

It wasn't *really* about hair. It was about healing. It was about surrender. It was about sacrifice. It was about acknowledging that my looks and my need to be comfortable in my own skin were not as important as focusing on restoration.

What's your metaphorical curling iron? What's something small but powerful that you can release today in pursuit of something greater?

What's one **short-term pleasure** you're willing to sacrifice for long-term success?

____

____

____

How will you **respond** when the sacrifices get tough or when doubt creeps in?

____

____

____

What is one **non-negotiable** commitment you can make starting today?

____

____

____

How will you measure your progress, even when the results aren't immediate?

____

____

____

Who will hold you accountable when things get hard?

____

____

____

Final Word: It's Not About Loss—It's About Legacy

My final sentiment about your daily offering is this: your sacrifice today isn't about loss. It's about choosing something greater instead of whatever it was that was holding you back.

As your PIVOT Coach, I see you. And if you took the time to complete even a few of the questions above, I know you're wrestling with something real. You're juggling responsibilities, battling self-doubt, and trying to create a future that feels aligned with who you truly are.

Some days, it probably feels like too much—too many choices, too many expectations, too much uncertainty. But let me remind you of this: growth doesn't require you to do more. It simply asks you to choose what matters most.

A good pivot isn't about handling the ball more on the court. It's about knowing when to stop, plant your foot, and choose the best direction for your next move.

The road to your best self isn't paved with perfection; it's built with intention. One choice. One habit. One decision at a time. You don't have to overhaul everything today. Just pick one thing—one distraction to release, one truth to believe, one "yes" to your future.

You are not behind. You are not too late. And you are absolutely capable.

The fact that you're here, taking time to reflect and recommit, tells me everything I need to know—you're already transforming.

So, take a deep breath. Trust yourself. And remember:

Sacrifice isn't about loss. It's about making space for the life you were meant to live.

Let today's sacrifice shape tomorrow's strength.

One Final Challenge: Who Are You Becoming?

Before you close this chapter, I've got one last challenge for you.

Every night, for the next 7 days, ask yourself these two questions:

- **What did I sacrifice today that made me better?**
- **If I keep making these same choices, who will I become in six months?**

You don't become great by accident.

You become who you train to be.

On the court.

At work.

In life.

The ball is in your hands. What will you do with it?

ATHLETE
Spotlight

🏀 Jimmy Butler
The Grind Behind the Game

Jimmy Butler, six-time NBA All-Star and leader of the Miami Heat, is not just respected for his talent—he's revered for his relentless work ethic, personal sacrifice, and commitment to the grind. From humble beginnings to becoming one of the league's most mentally tough and physically consistent players, Butler's career is built on choosing discipline over distractions, day after day.

> "If you don't sacrifice for what you want,
> what you want becomes the sacrifice."
> — Jimmy Butler

- Early Life Sacrifices: Butler was homeless at age 13. He bounced from house to house, couch to couch, with no guarantees—just grit. He didn't use his situation as an excuse. He used it as fuel.

- Daily Discipline: Known for his 3:30 A.M. workouts, Jimmy is often the first to arrive at the gym and the last to leave. He's said, "You can't become great by sleeping in."

- Sacrificed Cool for Consistency: While other players were chasing clout, Butler was building stamina. While others were coasting on talent, he was pushing through pain. He traded the spotlight for sweat equity.

- Leadership by Example: Whether dragging his team to the Finals as an underdog or opting out of social life to stay focused during the playoffs, Butler sacrifices comfort for the bigger picture.

Jimmy Butler didn't rise through the NBA ranks because of flash—he got there because he showed up. He gave up everything that didn't serve his goals and made his life about one thing: becoming better than he was yesterday.

Offering Prompts:

I already know—this part of your daily PIVOT Practice might stretch you more than the others. That's why I'm not leaving you to figure it out on your own.

Here's the truth: what you're willing to release today creates space for who you're becoming tomorrow. Some days, you'll offer up the same thing because the lesson's still working its way through. Other days, a brand-new challenge will meet you before noon—and with it, a brand-new cross to carry. But hear me when I say: **don't skip this step.**

Even the smallest daily sacrifice builds the muscle of discipline—and it moves you one decision closer to the life you say you want.

Use one of these prompts each morning to help you name your daily offering:

- What is one comfort or habit I can release today to move closer to my goal?
- What do I need to say "no" to today in order to say "yes" to my future?
- Where am I wasting time or energy that could be redirected with intention?
- What narrative or excuse do I need to surrender so I can finally take the next step?
- What craving (food, attention, validation, control) do I need to pause today so I can make room for better?
- What part of me am I pretending is "fine" that actually needs to be addressed and offered up for healing?

- What decision have I been putting off that I can face head-on today?
- What small act of discipline can I choose today to stay aligned with my bigger purpose?
- What emotional weight have I been carrying that I can lay down, even just for today?
- What fear can I surrender today, trusting that growth is on the other side?

Practice Drills: Identifying Your Daily Offering

In basketball, greatness isn't built on game day — it's built in practice. The same is true in life. Every day, you have a chance to sacrifice something small to gain something greater. Here I have given you four Practice Drills, which include:

- The Extra Mile Drill, for when you need to give a little bit more than your usual.
- The No Shortcuts Drill, for when you need to hold yourself accountable.
- The 1% Trade-Off Drill, to help you remember the power of tiny, intentional moves.
- The Mental Reset Drill, to retrain your brain on how to deal with disappointment or wrong moves.

These drills are designed to help you train your mind, character, and spirit, just like athletes train their bodies and skills. Use one per day or stretch one over an entire week. The goal? To build habits that move you forward, on and off the court.

YOUR DAILY DRILL

The Extra Mile Drill

Purpose

To strengthen your self-discipline and build a rock-solid work ethic.
This isn't about perfection - it's about showing up with intention
when it would be easier to tap out.

Life Application

Today, you are going to stretch yourself past what is comfortable. That means
finishing the project after your brain says, "I'm done." It means sending a thank-you
note when no one expects it. It means walking back into the conversation when
you'd rather shut down. You don't have to do everything.
But you do have to *do* one thing more than usual.

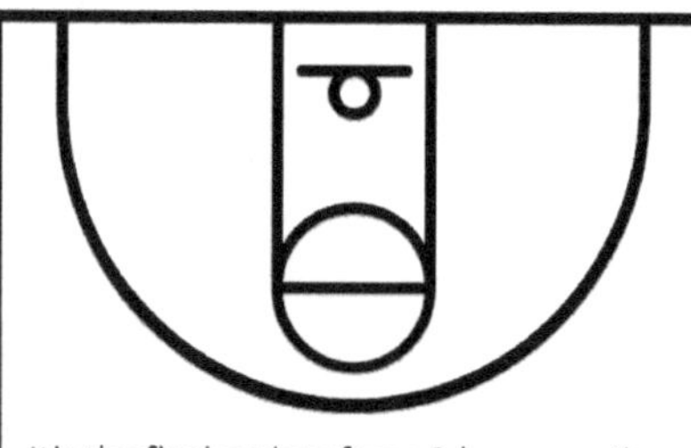

It's the final sprint after a 2-hour practice.
The last free throw after the buzzer. It's
doing the rep when your legs say no but
your heart says go.

Coach's Challenge

Today, set aside a daily
"extra".
One extra call.
One extra rep.
One extra page read.
One extra deep breath
before reacting.
Keep a daily tally for the
week.
Watch how consistency
compounds.

Lesson for Today

Champions aren't built in comfort.
They're forged in the decision to press forward
when every part of you says stop.
The extra mile is lonely, but it's where greatness lives.

YOUR DAILY DRILL

The No Shortcuts Drill

Purpose

To strengthen your integrity and personal responsibility.
This drill is about doing things the right way,
even when nobody's checking your work.
Especially then.

Life Application

You know the moment.
The one where you think, "No one will notice if I skip this step."
Whether it's not proofreading the email, returning the cart,
or letting someone else take the blame, you pause.
And instead of cutting corners, you choose character.
You complete the task with intention, not just completion.

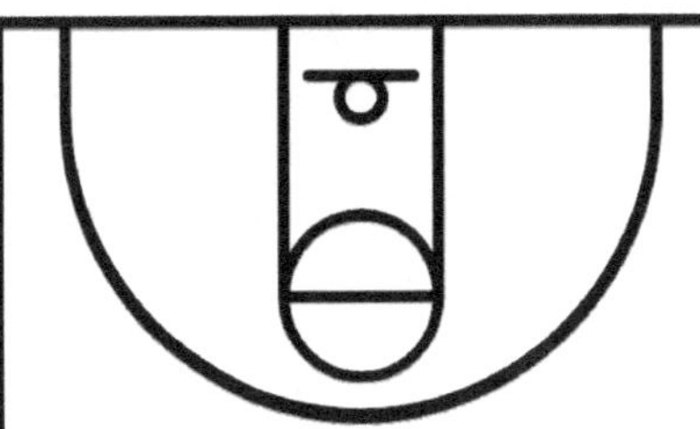

Touching every line during suicides.
Following through with the shot after the
whistle. Hustling like the coach is watching,
because character shows up when she isn't.

Coach's Challenge

Identify one task each day where you're tempted to rush or skip.

Finish it all the way through, with care, clarity, and no shortcuts. Log your completion moments for the week. Notice how your confidence and consistency grow.

Lesson for Today

The habits you form in secret shape the results you live in public.
Shortcuts shrink you. Integrity stretches you.
Excellence is a daily decision, not a once-in-a-while act.
Train it in.

YOUR DAILY DRILL

The 1% Trade-Off Drill

Purpose

To help you recognize the power of small, intentional sacrifices.
This drill is about choosing what to let go of today
so that you can step into the life you truly want tomorrow.

Life Application

This week, identify one thing you can give up—not forever,
just for now—that will create space for something better.
Maybe it's 30 fewer minutes on your phone,
skipping the fast food line, or trading late-night scrolling
for early-morning stillness.
It's not about perfection—it's about progress. Small trade-offs, big results.

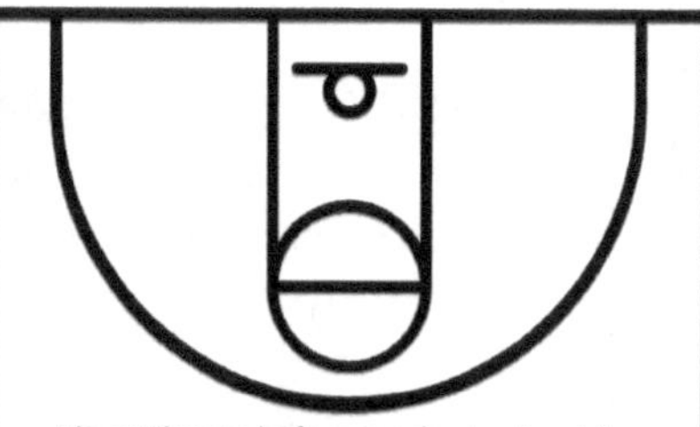

It's getting up before sunrise to shoot free throws while the world sleeps. It's picking extra conditioning over hanging out. It's sacrificing what's easy for what's necessary.

Coach's Challenge

**Pick one area of your life where you can sacrifice just 1% of comfort for 100% of clarity.
Journal it daily.
What did it trade? What did open up in return?
These 1% moments might seem small now, but they stack fast.**

Lesson for Today

Big wins are built on quiet, unseen choices.
The world celebrates leaps, but real transformation
happens 1% at a time.
Train yourself to make the trade, and trust the payoff.

The Mental Reset Drill

Purpose

To retrain how you respond to failure, frustration, and the unprecedented.
This drill is about breaking the spiral and choosing a better next move, on purpose.

Life Application

Today, when things go sideways—whether it's a missed deadline,
a snappy reply, or forgetting the appointment—stop.
Literally pause. Reset your posture. Inhale. Exhale.
Then say something out loud that puts you back in the game:
"I'm built for this." "Shake it off." "Next play."
You can't control every moment, but you can control your response to it.

You miss a shot. You lose the ball. You foul.
The greats don't hang their heads. They nod,
regroup, and get back into position.
They don't carry the mistake -
they carry the lesson.

Coach's Challenge

This week, track how many times you reset instead of react.

Create your own go-to phrase for setbacks. Write it on a sticky note. Put it on your mirror, your desktop, or your dashboard. Make it your mental anchor.

Lesson for Today

Failure isn't final - it's feedback.
The comeback starts the moment you reset your mind,
not when you fix the mistake.
Greatness doesn't dwell int he past.
It powers up for the next play.

6

T IS FOR TRAINING

Post-Op Doctor's Note:

Anthony returns today. He is now 4 weeks out. Pins are still in place. Pain is 3/10. Pins are in good position. We removed his remaining sutures today, applied a little bit of silver nitrate, and put a new dressing on. I want him to continue to change the dressing every 2-3 days. He can shower and let a little warm water run over his foot. X-rays needed at next visit. We will remove the pins on his next visit.

"IF YOU DON'T DO WHAT'S BEST FOR YOUR BODY, YOU'RE THE ONE WHO COMES UP ON THE SHORT END."
—ATTRIBUTED TO JULIUS ERVING

I f *prayer* is the foundation, *investigation* is your mind's food, *visualization* is your mental rehearsal, and *offering* is the daily sacrifice that stretches your capacity, then *training* is where it all gets physical.

This is where the pivot starts to move from theory to transformation. It's the practice. The grind. The reps. The part where you start becoming who you say you want to be.

But here's the deal: training isn't just about what you do with your body—it's also about what you do with your *mind.* Both need discipline. Both require practice. And both deserve their own spotlight.

That's why, for the first time in this playbook, we're splitting this into **two parts**:

1. Training the Body

2. Training the Mind

They're both critical. And they both matter—individually and together.

No, I'm not expecting you to start training for a marathon tomorrow or max out your bench press. But if you've ever spent a season of life avoiding exercise (or convincing yourself that "being busy" counts as cardio), it's time to pivot from that train of thought for the rest of this book.

After what we went through as a family, and after watching my son recover step by step—seeing him get back on the court just four months later, running faster than ever—I realized the connection between *physical transformation* and *mental strength* was undeniable.

I'm not sure where you are in your health journey, but let's be honest—everyone from doctors and scientists to little league coaches and curvy influencers on Instagram has reminded us how important it is to take care of our bodies. Can you relate?

I still hear my high school band director, Mr. Pantoja, shouting, "Carruth! Go get some water! Your face is too red for this Texas heat!" Or my dad, telling me to hop on my bike and "go get some exercise."

And of course, we all know the basics: eat a balanced diet with real food, stretch regularly, get enough sleep, don't skip breakfast, warm up before workouts, cool down after, and stay consistent. (Did I miss anything? Oh, portion control—especially hard when you're from Texas.)

So, take a deep breath. We're not trying to create the perfect routine. We're trying to create a sustainable one.

Let's start with the body—because once you start moving differently, you start thinking differently too.

Part 1—Training Your Body

The Truth About Training: Just Show Up

If you're reading this book, I'm not here to lecture you about working out every day. That's not my message. In fact, this is the very thing I wrestle with—365 days a year.

That's 18,250 days of inconsistent eating habits, roller-coaster workout routines, countless before-and-after photos (that I pray never resurface), and over 400,000 minutes obsessing about food and exercise that could've been spent on something that actually fueled my purpose.

Truth is, I've spent more energy focused on what I look like than on cultivating sustainable habits that actually make me feel good. I didn't create a wellness routine—I created a monster. One made up of inconsistency, chaos, and binge dieting masked as "getting back on track."

But something shifts when you become a parent—especially when your baby (even if he's nearly six feet tall) lives and breathes fitness and then suddenly gets sidelined by an injury. Watching my son go from athlete to patient was a wake-up call for both of us. He needed to rebuild, and so did I.

That's where the T in PIVOT comes in. T stands for **training and transformation**.

Because training is the bridge between *intention* and *transformation*.

It's the disciplined, daily practice of showing up—even when you don't feel like it.

You don't have to push yourself to the edge every day. You just have to *show up*.

Whether it's your body, your mind, or your spirit—*training is where growth gets activated.*

In the context of your PIVOT routine, training is about more than physical fitness—it's about preparing for your best life. It's not just about how you look in the mirror; it's about how you feel in your body, how you move through your day, and how you show up for what matters most.

Yes, I get it—we live in a world obsessed with aesthetics. Slim waists. Toned arms. Six-pack abs. But real transformation isn't about chasing a photo-ready version of yourself. It's about becoming strong enough, clear enough, and disciplined enough to live a full life—not just for today, but for decades to come.

This journey isn't about squeezing back into your college jeans (though if that's on your list—go for it!). It's about building the stamina to chase your kids around the house, the flexibility to kneel in prayer without pain, the energy to pour into your calling without burning out.

As we age, our bodies are either becoming more capable or more compromised. There is no neutral ground. If you don't train it, you lose it. Period. Strength training and cardio aren't just gym buzzwords—they're tools for sustaining your health, your confidence, and your freedom.

In Scripture, we're reminded in 1 Corinthians 9:27, "I discipline my body like an athlete, training it to do what it should." Paul wasn't just talking about physical conditioning—he was teaching us that our bodies, minds, and spirits must be aligned for us to fully live out our calling.

Your body isn't just a vessel; it's part of the divine strategy.

And when you train it—when you choose to move it, fuel it, and care for it—you're not just improving your health. You're reinforcing the mental and spiritual muscle it takes to live well, lead boldly, and pivot with power.

Athletes know this.

Consider legendary Chicago Bulls player Michael Jordan. Jordan didn't become great just because of his natural talent. He became great because he trained his body *and* his mind to show up every single day—whether it was game day or not. Long before the cameras flashed or the championship banners were raised, Jordan was in the gym. Early mornings. Late nights. Repetition. Sweat. Failure. And try again. He practiced harder than he played so that when the moment came, he didn't have to rise to the occasion—he could simply return to the level he had trained for.

Jordan famously said, "I can accept failure, everyone fails at something. But I can't accept not trying." That quote wasn't just a soundbite—it was a lifestyle. Jordan used mental rehearsal to prepare for every shot, every game-winning scenario, every "what if" that could unfold on the court. He visualized not only himself making the shot, but also every possible defender, every possible angle, every pressure-packed moment—and he trained for it.

His legendary trainer, Tim Grover, once shared that Jordan didn't just train for basketball. He trained to dominate. He worked on strength, speed, recovery, and even response time. But most importantly, he trained his mindset to remain relentless. His focus wasn't just on talent—it was on tenacity.

Then there's the Los Angeles Lakers great, Kobe Bryant. Kobe didn't train for the applause—he trained for the quiet hours. He was often in the gym by 4 a.m., lacing up his sneakers while most of the world was still asleep. While others were just beginning to stir, Kobe had already logged hours of focused work—drilling footwork, perfecting his shot, pushing his limits. He called it the *Mamba Mentality*—a mindset of relentless pursuit and radical preparation. What most people saw were the buzzer-beaters, the trophies, and the iconic moments. But what made those moments possible was the unseen grind—the countless mornings he beat the sunrise, the deliberate way he visualized each movement before executing it, and the daily decision to outwork not just his competitors, but his own excuses.

Kobe wasn't just training his body—he was training his *will*. That kind of commitment doesn't just produce physical transformation. It rewires the brain. It builds a kind of mental resilience that allows you to push past fatigue, failure, and fear. It creates muscle memory for greatness—so that even in high-pressure moments, your response is automatic, because your preparation was intentional.

This is the power of daily training. This is the quiet work behind every bold pivot. Kobe once said, "Great things come from hard work and perseverance. No excuses." And that's a truth you can carry with you. Because the transformation you seek doesn't start in the spotlight—it starts in the silence. It starts when no one is watching. It starts when you choose to show up anyway.

And in the world of tennis, Serena Williams' training was the stuff used for documentaries and movies. Her physical training regimen is legendary—but it's her *mental toughness* that truly sets her apart. We've watched her dominate courts, rewrite history books, and come back from injury, loss, and life-altering moments. But behind every title and trophy is a woman who refused to let setbacks define her.

Williams once said, "I really think a champion is defined not by their wins but by how they can recover when they fall." That's more than a quote—it's her testimony. Because Serena has fallen. Publicly. Painfully. She's faced devastating injuries, a life-threatening postpartum experience, and waves of criticism no matter how many times she proved herself. And yet—she recovered. Not just physically, but mentally. Spiritually. Holistically. That's what makes her a true champion. (Can I just pause here and say to you: you have a champion inside of you, too.)

Her training was never just about strength and speed—it was about *focus, resilience*, and *belief*. She visualized her serve, her stance, her rhythm. But she also visualized how to get back up—how to keep playing through pain, how to silence doubt, and how to show up as her full self in spaces that weren't built for her. She trained her mind to meet every moment with fierce grace and fire.

And that's something we all need when life pivots on us. When you've been overlooked. Undervalued. When you've taken the hit and you're trying to figure out how to rise. Serena's story reminds us that recovery is just as much a discipline as the grind. It takes work to get back up. It takes vision to see yourself beyond the fall.

Whether you're stepping back onto a literal court or simply trying to find your way after a loss—Serena teaches us this: your comeback is greater than your stumble. It's how champions are made—not just in the arena, but in the quiet work of seeing themselves whole, healed, and victorious before the world ever catches on. These athletes weren't just training their bodies—they were building the kind of resilience that carries you through the unseen moments of life.

I've had seasons like that, too.

In my 20s, I was the definition of driven. Remember, I was a self-proclaimed gym rat. (No offense to my fellow gym-goers. We really did call ourselves that back in the

'90s.) I taught step aerobics five days a week in full glam and Reebok high-tops, followed strict meal plans, and trained like my dreams depended on it—because, in many ways, they did. I had real aspirations of becoming a professional fitness competitor. I tracked everything—macros, sleep, reps, even self-doubt.

And yes, I really did write to Arnold Schwarzenegger when I was 23, asking him to sponsor me for a fitness competition in Hollywood. I didn't just believe in my goals—I chased them with the kind of boldness that didn't need permission. I was fearless. Or maybe just too focused to notice fear at all.

But life evolves.

In my 30s, I transitioned into a new season: wife, mother, professional, nurturer, caretaker, career builder. And somewhere between diaper bags and boardrooms, I noticed my priorities shifting. My energy wasn't going toward sculpting abs—it was going toward building a life.

And maybe that's where you are, too. You're not trying to crush a personal record—you're trying to crush your to-do list and still have energy left for yourself.

Let me remind you: physical training isn't about perfection. It's about movement. You don't need an hour at the gym. You need ten minutes of commitment to yourself. A walk around the block. A stretch break between Zoom meetings. A dance party with your kids in the kitchen. These moments count.

My workouts weren't happening in a gym anymore—they were showing up in my daily commitment to myself, my family, and the promises God placed on my heart.

That's when I began to understand something deeper: transformation isn't just about what you can do with your body—it's about what you decide to do with your mind. And as much as I loved the thrill of hitting a new personal best, I learned that true growth doesn't happen in performance—it happens in practice. In the quiet, messy, unglamorous moments when you decide to keep showing up.

I don't teach this PIVOT Routine from a place of theory. I've lived it. I've had to reimagine who I was becoming multiple times—on the mat, off the stage, and in every chapter where life didn't look like I thought it would.

So, whether you're a former gym rat like I was, a busy mom trying to reclaim her energy, or a woman navigating yet another unexpected transition—I see you. And more importantly, I know you can do this.

Time to Plan Your Reps

Let's get honest, intentional, and a little bit uncomfortable (that's where the growth is, right?). I want us to reflect on where your body needs more attention—and how small, consistent movement can become one of your most powerful forms of transformation.

How have your priorities around your health and energy shifted over the years? Be honest—has it been about how you look... like me... or how you feel?

____

____

____

____

What area of your physical life feels the most out of alignment right now—movement, sleep, nutrition, hydration, rest?

____

____

____

____

Where in your day can you realistically carve out 5, maybe even 10, minutes just for your body? (Pro Tip: if you have time to scroll for this long, you've got time.)

____

____

____

____

What's one small movement habit you can commit to for the next 7 days? (Be specific—"walk for 10 minutes after lunch" beats "exercise more.")

____

____

____

____

____

How does your body feel when you're energized and rested?

____

____

____

How does your physical energy (or lack of it) affect your confidence, clarity, or focus?

____

____

____

Who in your life will benefit when you start showing up with more strength, energy, and presence? (Yes, your wellness has a ripple effect!)

____

____

____

____

Be sure you write your answers down and revisit them this week. Your transformation and training start in these small, intentional steps.

Be Intentional

By now, I hope you've taken a few moments to reflect. Go back, revisit your answers, and sit with them this week. Your transformation doesn't start in the gym—it starts in small, consistent, intentional steps.

Let's talk about how we make that happen.

Being a mom (or a dad) is a full-time job. Once you become a parent, you're never not one, right? It's a 24/7 assignment. And for many of us—including me—a job outside the home was necessary, too. During the first 18 years of parenting, I couldn't find five minutes for myself if they were gift-wrapped and dropped on my doorstep. And if you're a parent, I bet you've felt the same.

(But even if you're not a parent, stay with me—I see you. You've got responsibilities, deadlines, pressure, and expectations, too. And this message is just as much for you.)

That's where *intentionality* becomes everything.

Your PIVOT routine becomes a solid anchor—a practice you can return to no matter how crazy your schedule gets. Just five minutes each:

- Five minutes of prayer.
- Five minutes of investigation.
- Five minutes of visualization.
- Five minutes of offering something up.
- And five minutes of training—your body or your mind.

That's 25 minutes to reset your day. You've got that. I promise.

In my 30s, I became a wife and mom. And somewhere along the way, my 20-something abs quietly clocked out—replaced by a softer, rounder version that looked a lot like the chubby little girl I used to be in Texas. Spoiler alert: Chasing a toddler doesn't burn as many calories as step aerobics and protein shakes.

I didn't have the time—or energy—to focus on me. That's when the migraines started. The anxiousness crept in. My finances took a hit because I was constantly buying bigger clothes. My marriage struggled. My health slipped. And I didn't know how to get back to the girl I used to be.

In my 40s, I tried. The weight leveled out, but the habits still lagged. Starting over felt so much harder than it had in my 20s. But the truth? I could have carved out five minutes every day. Had I known better, I would have started smaller.

And that's exactly why I created *The PIVOT Principle.* Because now, in my 50s, this daily practice has become my lifeline—not just to better physical health, but to better mental strength and spiritual peace. I'm not perfect at it. And you won't be either. But progress doesn't require perfection—just intention.

5 Steps to Reclaiming Your Energy (One Day at a Time)

Here's how to get intentional with your training:

1. Commit to Movement Daily

   This isn't about marathons—it's about momentum. Walk. Stretch. Lift. Dance. Cycle. Whatever moves your body with purpose. Start with five minutes. Let it grow from there. On days I don't feel like it, I literally set a timer for five minutes and go.

   Did I enjoy it? Not always.

   But did I feel proud afterward because I kept my promise to myself? Absolutely.

2. Train Your Thoughts

    Like your muscles, your mind needs reps too. Practice gratitude. Speak truth. Interrupt those negative thought loops and replace them with what's actually true. Philippians 4:8 reminds us to think on things that are "true, noble, and praiseworthy." That's not just spiritual advice—it's mental conditioning.

3. Fuel Like You Mean It

    Fuel isn't just food—it's everything you consume. Eat to energize. Consume content that lifts your spirit. Spend time around people who fill you, not drain you. And be still long enough to hear your own thoughts.

4. Rest Strategically

    Even Jesus rested. Even Olympians nap. Rest isn't weakness—it's wisdom. So, take the nap. Log it in your journal and celebrate that you honored your limits. Rest is how you refill what you've poured out.

5. Track the Wins

    Every rep counts. Every walk, every water bottle finished, every mindset shift. Write them down. Celebrate the small stuff. That's how you build sustainable habits—and how transformation becomes a lifestyle.

You don't need a gym membership. You need a reset. A reminder that movement matters, that your body is worth showing up for, and that training is more than just exercise—it's a declaration: *I'm not giving up on me.*

Transformation isn't a one-time event. It's a daily decision to show up, train up, and trust God with the results.

So, lace up. Grab your journal. Press play on that playlist.

Let's get back to you.

Training Your Body—Five Minutes at a Time

Let's be real—when life gets busy, even thinking about a 60-minute workout can feel like trying to climb Mount Everest in heels. But here's the truth:

Transformation doesn't require a gym membership, high-end leggings, or two hours of your day.

It just takes five intentional minutes. That's it. Five minutes to move, stretch, sweat, or breathe with purpose.

And this isn't just motivational fluff—the science backs it up.

A 2025 study from Edith Cowan University showed that just five minutes of slow, controlled movements (like squats or wall push-ups) can lead to real gains in strength, flexibility, and even mental clarity. These "eccentric" exercises don't require any equipment—meaning, you can do them in your living room, office, or hotel room. No excuses.

Columbia University researchers also found that a five-minute walk every 30 minutes during long periods of sitting dramatically lowers blood pressure and blood sugar. Think about that: five minutes of movement isn't just symbolic—it's powerful. It shifts things inside your body in real-time.

That's what I love most about the PIVOT Routine:

It meets you where you are.

It's not about perfection—it's about motion. Progress. Presence. Five focused minutes that shift your body and remind your mind that you're still in the game.

When Anthony began his recovery, we didn't start with sprints or suicides. We started with what we had—slow, steady laps. Taking the stairs. Light stretches. Movement that was intentional, doable, and consistent. And I realized—I could do the same.

We weren't training for a championship. We were training for life—to rebuild strength, confidence, and trust in our bodies again.

So, I joined him.

I committed to five minutes a day.

Some days it was strength training.

Other days, a walk, a stretch, or dancing around the living room like nobody was watching (and thank God they weren't).

And you know what?

It worked.

As I write in this chapter, I'm down 18 pounds. Not because I overhauled my entire life overnight, but because I chose to show up—for five minutes—over and over again.

Here's what I've learned:

You don't have to go hard.

You just have to go.

Five minutes is all it takes to remind your body—and your brain—that you're in motion. That you're choosing transformation. That you're not done yet.

It starts here.

One intentional step at a time.

ATHLETE
Spotlight

 **Dwayne "The Rock" Johnson**
The Power of Physical Discipline

You may know Dwayne "The Rock" Johnson for his blockbuster movies, but before Hollywood, he was grinding it out in the weight room. A former college football player turned pro wrestler, Johnson built his global brand not just with talent, but through a training ethic that's legendary.

His 4 a.m. gym sessions—whether filming, traveling, or on vacation—are part of his non-negotiable routine. For The Rock, training isn't just about looking strong—it's about being strong, inside and out.

> "Success isn't always about greatness.
> It's about consistency. Consistent hard work gains success.
> Greatness will come."
> – Dwayne Johnson

He's open about how fitness transformed his life—not just physically, but mentally and emotionally. Johnson has shared how workouts helped him navigate depression, career disappointments, and personal setbacks.

- Training is his daily anchor.
- He approaches fitness as a form of self-mastery and resilience.
- His routine is built on discipline, not motivation.

PIVOT Connection: The Rock reminds us that transformation isn't a one-time decision—it's a daily, deliberate commitment to show up for yourself. And that commitment starts with training.

Training Prompts: Small Moves that Make a Big Difference

You don't need a gym membership, a perfect body, or a full hour to train. You just need five intentional minutes. Try one of these prompts each day to get moving without over-thinking it. Keep it simple. Keep it consistent. Keep it honest.

1. Walk during your lunch break—around the building, up and down the stairs, or just out to your car and back.

2. Set a timer every hour to stand up, stretch, and do 20 air squats or wall push-ups.

3. While on a conference call, do 5 minutes of calf raises, marches in place, or seated leg lifts.

4. Replace 5 minutes of scrolling with a quick dance break to your favorite song—yes, seriously.

5. Do slow bodyweight squats or leg swings as you wait for your coffee or dinner to finish.

6. Before your shift or after your nap, stretch out your back and hips with 3 simple yoga poses.

7. Do a walking lap inside your home every commercial break or podcast ad.

8. Play your "hype song" and do 3 minutes of jumping jacks, knee lifts, or shoulder rolls.

9. Hold a 60-second plank while your kids brush their teeth—challenge yourself daily.

10. March in place or jog around the living room during cartoons or clean-up time.

11. Turn clean-up time into cardio: squat to pick up toys, lunge across the room, or dance with the broom.

12. Do 10 reps of push-ups (on the counter or the floor) every time you enter the kitchen.

13. Wake up 10 minutes earlier and commit to a full-body circuit: squats, lunges, push-ups, repeat.

14. Turn a 10-minute walk into a mindful practice: breathe deeply, stretch halfway through, and thank your body as you move.

15. Use your evenings to unwind with intentional movement—foam roll, stretch, or follow a gentle YouTube mobility video.

16. Set a weekly "movement date" with yourself—just you and your goal, even if it's in your pajamas.

Remember: The goal isn't perfection—it's participation. Five intentional minutes a day can shift your mood, your mindset, and your momentum. Choose one prompt. Show up. And let that small win lead to bigger strength.

Practice Drills: Train like Your Life Depends on It (Because It Kind of Does)

Just like on the court, progress comes from practice. These drills are meant to help you train your body with intention, one rep and one rhythm at a time. You don't need fancy equipment—just a little space, a timer, and a decision to show up.

Drill #1: 5-Minute AMRAP (As Many Rounds As Possible)

Set a timer for 5 minutes. Repeat the following circuit:

- 10 squats
- 10 wall push-ups
- 10 alternating lunges (or step-backs)
- 10 jumping jacks (or high knees if low impact)

Why it works: You build momentum fast. Short bursts create quick wins.

Drill #2: The "Pivot Stretch" Sequence

Perfect after a long day or first thing in the morning. Flow through each move for 30 seconds to 1 minute:

- Neck rolls
- Shoulder circles
- Cat-cow stretch
- Forward fold
- Hip openers
- Seated twist

Why it works: It opens up tension and reminds your body it's safe to move again.

Drill #3: Commercial Break Burner

While watching TV (or listening to a podcast), use commercial breaks or 3-minute pauses to:

- Hold a plank
- Do leg lifts while seated
- March in place or do side steps
- Calf raises at the kitchen counter

Why it works: No extra time needed—just intentionality.

Drill #4: Walk & Talk

Call a friend or play a voice memo of encouragement while walking outside or pacing your house. 10 minutes. No scrolling allowed.

Why it works: Moves your body and boosts your mindset.

Drill #5: Name-Your-Why Workout

Write your "why" on a sticky note. Place it in your workout space. Every rep you do—say it aloud or in your mind.

Example: "I move for energy." "I move for healing." "I move for my kids."

Set a timer and go.

Why it works: Puts purpose behind the practice.

Drill #6: Movement Ladder

Choose one movement (e.g., squats or jumping jacks).

Start with 1 rep. Add 1 rep every round until you hit 10. Then work your way back down.

Takes 5–7 minutes. Build intensity as you climb.

Why it works: Creates a mental and physical finish line—and you'll feel powerful by the end.

Coach's Note from Dr. Shelley:

You don't need to "feel ready" to start. Readiness grows with repetition. These drills are about showing up for yourself on purpose—not proving anything to anyone else. Give yourself five minutes. Trust the process. You're in training for the life you've prayed for.

Part 2—Training Your Mind

If your body needs movement, your mind craves stillness. Peace. Calm. Just as muscles grow through repetition, your thoughts gain clarity and resilience through consistent, intentional practice.

And here's what most people get wrong: **Training your mind isn't about silencing your thoughts—it's about stewarding them.** This, too, is, in my opinion, the major difference between mindfulness practices originating from Buddhism and mindfulness practices rooted in Christ. It's about tuning in, noticing without judgment, and gently guiding your attention back to what matters most.

As a Certified Mindfulness Trainer, I've seen how powerful this practice is—not just on paper, but in real life. And no, I don't sit cross-legged on a mountaintop. I sit in traffic. I juggle schedules. I navigate job loss, motherhood, deadlines, and doubt—just like you. But I've also seen how five minutes of intentional stillness can shift everything.

Transformation Truths for Training the Mind

Let's ground this next level of your journey in truth—because mindset isn't just a buzzword. It's the battleground. And the way you train your thoughts will either elevate or limit your life.

Truth #1: Discipline is more powerful than motivation.

Motivation fades. Discipline shows up anyway.

When I set my sights on becoming a fitness competitor, I was all in. Highly motivated. Hyper-focused. I had the meal plans, the gym routine, the vision board, and even the letter to Arnold Schwarzenegger to prove it. And for a while, that motivation carried me far.

But here's what I learned: motivation has a shelf life. It spikes when the goal is new, when the vision feels fresh, or when someone notices your progress. But eventually, life kicks in—schedules shift, stress builds, and that initial fire starts to dim. And when my motivation faded? So did the regimen. Because my discipline wasn't strong enough to carry the weight when my motivation couldn't.

This is what separates those who dabble from those who commit. Take Kobe Bryant, for example. He didn't get up at 4 a.m. because he was always motivated—he did it because he had a system. A standard. Bryant once said, "I don't negotiate with myself." It wasn't about waiting to feel ready. It was about deciding ahead of time and honoring that decision.

So, here's what I want you to remember: you don't need to feel like it to be consistent. You just need to show up. Even for five minutes. Let discipline take the lead—because that's where the real transformation begins.

Truth #2: Your body follows where your mind goes.

Change your thinking, change your habits—change your life.

Let's be real—most of the time, we think transformation starts with action. But in reality, it starts in the mind. You can have the best intentions in the world, but if your thoughts are stuck in fear, doubt, or defeat, your body will follow that lead every single time.

I've lived this. On the days when I told myself I was too busy, too tired, or too behind to make progress, guess what? I didn't move. I didn't eat well. I didn't take care of myself. My body followed the story I was telling myself. And it wasn't until I started interrupting that internal dialogue—catching the lie and replacing it with truth—that things actually began to shift.

Here's where mindfulness starts to come into play. Mindfulness teaches us that we are not our thoughts—but we do have the power to notice them, interrupt them, and redirect them. Your thoughts are not facts—they're patterns. And patterns can be changed. This is why training your mind is just as important as training your body. If your thoughts are rooted in defeat, you'll move through your day like you've already lost. But if your thoughts are rooted in possibility, your actions will start aligning with progress—even in small, powerful ways.

Think about Serena Williams. She didn't dominate the game just because of her serve—she trained herself mentally to recover from criticism, injury, and personal loss. She taught herself how to think like a champion, not just play like one. When she stepped on the court, her body knew what to do because her mind had already rehearsed the victory.

So here's your nudge: want a better outcome? Start with a better thought. We'll dig deeper into mindfulness later in this chapter, but for now—just start paying attention. What are you rehearsing in your mind? Is it peace or pressure? Victory or defeat?

Because the truth is—your body is listening. And it will go wherever your mind tells it to.

Truth #3: Progress happens in the practice, not the performance.

You're not failing just because it's hard. You're growing because you're doing it.

Think about your career. How much of what you do every day came from a textbook or a certification course? Maybe 20%—if that. The real learning? It happened on the job. In the meetings where things went off-script. In the client conversations that didn't follow the slides. In the moments when you had to figure it out in real time and stay calm under pressure. That's where your growth happened—not in the training, but in the doing.

Training your mind works the same way. Reading this book, listening to sermons, completing professional development hours—those are all good. But transformation doesn't happen when you absorb information. It happens when you apply it. When you practice it. When you take what you've learned and put it to work in the middle of your messy, real-life situations.

Even elite athletes don't rise to the occasion—they return to the level of their training. And that training isn't glamorous. It's repetitive. It's quiet. It's done when no one is watching. But it's what makes the difference in the moment that counts.

So, if you're struggling right now—if the habit feels hard, if the new rhythm isn't second nature yet—don't assume you're failing. Assume you're training. You're building a new mental muscle. And just like any skill on the job, it takes repetition to get it right.

Because real progress doesn't show up in the big presentation—it shows up in the daily reps that got you there. And every time you show up for yourself in practice, you're preparing for the next breakthrough.

Truth #4: Life is the gym.

You don't need a studio—you need a shift. The way you respond to adversity is the real workout.

We don't always get to choose our circumstances, but we always get to choose how we respond. That's where the real mental training happens—not when everything's peaceful and perfectly aligned, but when the schedule blows up, when the answer is "no," or when the rug gets pulled out from under you.

You don't need a designated space, a fitness tracker, or even a quiet moment to train your mind. You train in real time. In carpool lines, in conflict, during the job search, after the breakup. Those moments? That's life spotting you while you build endurance.

It's a lot like preparing for a storm. You don't wait until the winds are howling to buy batteries or board up windows. You prepare when the skies are still calm. So, when adversity shows up—because it will—you've already built the mindset that can withstand it.

And here's the good news: we're not alone in that training. Romans 5:3–4 reminds us that "suffering produces perseverance; perseverance, character; and character, hope." That's not just a feel-good verse—it's a spiritual training plan. It tells us that every rep of resistance—every challenge, delay, or frustration—is actually strengthening something deeper in us. Not just endurance, but character. Not just toughness, but hope.

This is why I say life is the gym. The commute becomes the classroom. The argument becomes the test. The setback becomes the resistance band that strengthens your resilience.

So don't discount your everyday stressors. They're not just distractions. They're training tools. And your response is your rep.

You don't have to wait for the perfect environment to start strengthening your mindset. You're already in it. The gym is open. And God is your Trainer.

Athletes Train Their Minds, Too

If you've made it this far, you've already seen how discipline shaped legends like Jordan, Kobe, and Serena. But here's something we often overlook: their greatness wasn't just built in the gym or on the court—it was cultivated in their minds.

Michael Jordan didn't just practice buzzer-beaters—he mentally rehearsed making the shot with precision. Over and over again. In his head before it ever happened in real life. That way, when the pressure hit, it wasn't a surprise—it was muscle memory.

Kobe Bryant was famous for visualizing entire games in advance. Every screen, every defender, every clutch moment—he mentally played them out before his sneakers ever hit the hardwood. His mind was prepared long before the lights came on.

Serena Williams didn't just rely on power and skill—she built mental reset routines into her matches. Between sets, she would breathe deeply, recenter, and prepare herself to stay locked in, even when the pressure skyrocketed.

Even Laurie Hernandez, one of the youngest gymnasts to win Olympic gold, credited her ability to stay calm on the mat to her use of positive affirmations. She trained her self-talk to be louder than her fear.

And this isn't just old-school sports talk anymore.

These days, most professional teams don't just have strength coaches—they have performance psychologists, mental conditioning specialists, and mindset coaches. Entire departments are dedicated to training the brain. Why? Because they know something critical:

Your brain is the command center. If it breaks down under pressure, the body will follow.

Elite athletes train their minds to thrive under stress, not collapse under it. They rehearse success, yes—but they also practice how to respond to failure. They visualize comeback moments. They train for grit. For grace. For mental recovery.

They know that confidence isn't built when the crowd is cheering. It's built in the silence before the spotlight.

And if the most elite performers in the world are investing this much energy into strengthening their mindset... shouldn't we?

While we're on the subject, what are your thoughts on using a mindset coach? Take a few minutes and write down your thoughts here on the idea of having your very own coach.

____

____

____

____

____

Whether you have a personal coach or not, remember: you don't need a championship to train like a champion. You can hire your own coach. You can read a book like this and become your own coach. Really, you just need to start with five intentional minutes and the willingness to begin.

Mindfulness: Mental Training in Real Life

Before we go any further, let's be real about something we all do.

Have you ever driven home after a long day at work and pulled into the driveway... only to realize you don't even remember the drive? Like, at all? You stopped at red lights, changed lanes, maybe even waved at the neighbor— but your mind? Completely somewhere else.

Or how about this one: You're tearing through the house looking for your car keys, sunglasses, or phone—

only to find it exactly where you left it. Right there on the kitchen counter. Right in your hand. Right under your nose.

That, my friend, is what living on autopilot looks like. And we've all been there.

That's why this next part of your training matters so much. Because mindfulness isn't some fluffy buzzword reserved for yoga instructors or mountain retreats. It's mental training for real life.

Let's bust the myth now: mindfulness isn't about emptying your thoughts—it's about centering them. It's the ability to be still on purpose, to observe your thoughts without being run over by them.

It's not about zoning out. It's about tuning in.

And just like training your body, training your mind takes practice. A rhythm. A few small reps every day.

You don't need incense, a fancy meditation cushion, or a silent retreat in Bali (although that would be super nice, and I am not opposed to experiencing a little beachside getaway). You need five intentional minutes. That's it.

- Five minutes of breathing before you open your in-box.
- Five minutes of journaling your thoughts instead of scrolling your feed.
- Five minutes of prayer before you tackle that meeting or conflict or heavy decision.

Mindfulness is the daily discipline of choosing presence over pressure.

It's how you return to clarity when the world—and your brain—feel like they're spinning out.

So, before we dive into the how, take a breath. This isn't about doing more. It's about being more aware of what you're already doing.

Because transformation doesn't just happen in motion.

It happens in the pause.

The Science Behind the Stillness

This isn't just feel-good talk—this is brain science. Real, measurable, biological change. And it happens in stillness.

A Harvard study found that just eight weeks of mindfulness training led to visible changes in the brain. Participants experienced:

- Increased gray matter in the hippocampus (the area linked to learning, memory, and emotional regulation).
- Reduced activity in the amygdala (the fear and anxiety center).
- More calm, better focus, and a noticeable reduction in emotional reactivity.

That's not just a mindset shift. That's neuroplasticity—your brain rewiring itself through practice.

So, when I say five intentional minutes can change your day—and your life—I'm not being poetic. I'm being practical. You train your body at the gym. But your mind? It needs reps, too.

Athletes know this.

Novak Djokovic, one of the greatest tennis players of all time, credits mindfulness with helping him stay emotionally grounded and focused under pressure. He begins each day with breathwork, prayer, journaling, and meditation—not to perform better, but to live better. "It's more than just training for tennis," he said. "It's training for life."

And then there's George Mumford—the man behind the mental game of some of the biggest names in basketball. When Phil Jackson was coaching the Chicago Bulls in the '90s, he brought George onto the team to teach mindfulness to Jordan, Pippen, and the rest of the roster. Jackson later took Mumford with him to the Lakers, because he knew: if you want champions, you've got to train their minds.

In *The Mindful Athlete*, George writes, "When you are playing in the zone, your ego is out of the way, and you are totally in the moment. You're not thinking about the crowd, the score, or your stats. You're just doing."

Let's pause right there—because this applies to your life, too.

You're not on a basketball court, but you're in the game of life. So, what does "just doing" look like in your day?

- It's being fully present in the meeting instead of mentally rewriting your to-do list.
- It's choosing to breathe before you respond to your child, your partner, or that email.
- It's cooking dinner and actually noticing the texture, the smell, the movement of your hands.
- It's driving home from work and remembering the drive—because you weren't lost in your thoughts.
- It's hearing yourself think before the noise of the world rushes in at 7 a.m.

That's mindfulness. That's you in the zone.

When you're tuned in, you're not worried about how much is left on your plate. You're focused on the one thing you're doing right now. Your ego isn't running the show. Your presence is.

And you don't need a mat or a monastery. You need a moment.

That's what George Mumford taught champions. That's what I want you to practice.

Because the real game? It's not out there. It's inside. And when you train your mind to meet the moment with clarity, grace, and stillness—you win.

Bringing It All Together: Mindfulness as Mental Strength

Let's face it: life doesn't slow down just because we need a minute. But if we've learned anything from the greats—on the court, on the field, or in our own homes—it's that performance is only half the story. The real game is played in the mind.

That's why mental training matters.

It's why athletes like Jordan, Kobe, Serena, and Novak made it part of their daily routine. It's why coaches and teams now invest in performance psychologists and mindfulness coaches—because they understand this truth: the strongest bodies can still break down under pressure, but a trained mind knows how to steady the ship.

When Phil Jackson led the Bulls and later the Lakers, he didn't just build championship teams—he built centered teams. He understood that greatness isn't just about talent; it's about focus, presence, and the ability to stay grounded in high-pressure moments. That same principle applies to us. You don't have to be on a professional court to recognize your ability to remain present—especially in the chaos—is what sets you apart.

You don't need a spotlight to show up strong. You just need a rhythm that keeps you anchored.

So, the next time your thoughts start racing—when you realize you can't remember the drive home or you're searching for something that's been in plain sight—pause. Breathe. That's your moment. That's your training ground.

Because the truth is:

- Your mind is always training—either toward chaos or clarity.
- You can't control every thought, but you can choose how you respond to it.
- With just five intentional minutes a day, you can shift from running on empty to living on purpose.

This isn't about perfection. It's about presence.

Because when your body and your mind work together, you show up stronger. You think more clearly. You live better.

So today, whether you're stretching after your shower, sipping tea in silence, or whispering a prayer before bed—know that you are in training.

You are becoming.

This is your PIVOT.

ATHLETE
Spotlight

Cam F Awesome
Mental Strength Starts Young

Cam F Awesome isn't just a boxer—he's a mindset machine.
As a multi-time USA National Champion and Olympic Team member, Cam built his career not only by throwing punches, but by mastering his mind.

Growing up, Cam was bullied—his weight, his name, and his quiet nature all made him a target. But instead of becoming bitter, he got better. He joined a boxing gym, not just to learn how to fight, but to build confidence and mental control. That gym became the place where he transformed his mindset from fearful to fearless.

> "Your mindset controls your performance.
> I trained my mind long before I ever stepped in a ring."
> – Cam F Awesome

Today, Cam travels the country speaking to students and athletes about discipline, resilience, and mental health. He teaches that success isn't just about physical training—it's about controlling your thoughts and managing your emotions.

- Cam's story is about transformation through mental training.
- He developed emotional intelligence and inner peace to match his physical ability.
- He's proof that mental reps are just as powerful as physical ones.

PIVOT Connection: Cam's journey reflects the "T" in PIVOT—training your thoughts to shape your reality, even when your past says you shouldn't win.

Mental Training Prompts

Five intentional minutes is all it takes to shift your mind from reactive to resilient. Try one of these today:

1. Do a 5-Minute Box Breathing Session

    Inhale for 4 seconds, hold for 4, exhale for 4, hold for 4—repeat for 5 minutes to calm your nervous system.

2. Complete a Word Puzzle, Sudoku, or Brain Teaser

    Training your focus with a simple mental challenge builds memory, patience, and problem-solving skills.

3. Practice a Gratitude Blitz

    List 10 things you're grateful for—without overthinking. This trains your brain to scan for joy, not stress.

4. Try a Guided Visualization

    Close your eyes and picture your best self walking into a situation you've been dreading—confident, calm, clear.

5. Journal a "Mental Download"

    Write down everything on your mind for 3–5 minutes. No structure, no judgment—just a brain detox.

6. Name 5 Things You Can See, Hear, Touch, Smell, Taste

    This grounding technique helps bring your thoughts out of anxiety and back into the present moment.

7. Repeat a Scripture or Affirmation Aloud

   Choose one truth (e.g., "I have the mind of Christ" or "I am grounded, focused, and enough") and say it out loud for 2–3 minutes.

8. Write a Micro-Prayer

   "God, help me think clearly." "God, give me peace." Writing or whispering a simple prayer invites divine alignment.

9. Try a 3-Minute "Notice & Name" Walk

   Walk slowly and name everything you notice—colors, sounds, textures. It refocuses your brain from busy to aware.

10. Sketch or Color a Simple Pattern

    Use lines, circles, or colors to express your mental state. Creative mindfulness is both expressive and regulating.

11. Do a Scripture Meditation

    Choose one verse and reflect on every word. Write down what it reveals or how it applies to your current thoughts.

12. Declutter One Small Area

    Clear your desk, drawer, or email inbox. Physical clarity often brings mental clarity.

13. Turn Off All Noise for 5 Minutes

    No phone, no music, no podcast. Just be. Let your thoughts surface—and breathe through them.

14. Write a Letter to Your Future Self

    Envision who you want to become in 6 months or a year. What habits did he or she build? How does he or she think?

15. Ask Yourself a Centering Question

    Try: "What do I need right now?" or "What thought do I need to release today?" and journal the answer.

Practice Drills: Training Your Mind a Little Every Day

Choose something every day. Use one each day or apply it to an entire week.

- Drill 1: The 5-Minute Thought Cleanse

    Set a timer. Sit quietly and write down every thought that comes to mind—no editing, no structure. Then cross out anything rooted in fear, shame, or negativity. Rewrite one of those into a truth you can live by.

- Drill 2: Gratitude Rewire

    At the start or end of the day, list three things you're thankful for—specifically from today. This rewires your brain to search for goodness in real time.

- Drill 3: Scripture Reset

    Pick a verse (like Psalm 46:10 or Philippians 4:8). Say it aloud. Whisper it slowly. Write it three times. Let it replace whatever noise is dominating your mind today.

- Drill 4: Box Breathing Under Pressure

- Drill 5: Replace the Loop

Catch one negative or anxious thought during the day. Stop. Say out loud, "That's not the story I'm sticking with." Then speak better thoughts on purpose.

- Drill 6: The One-Thing Focus

Choose one task to give your full attention—no multitasking. Whether it's washing dishes, replying to an email, or having a conversation—be fully present. Notice the difference.

- Drill 7: The Intentional Input

Replace 10 minutes of mindless scrolling with 10 minutes of purposeful content: a podcast, a devotional, or one chapter of a book that builds you up.

- Drill 8: Mindful Movement

As you move your body (stretching, walking, exercising), tune into your breath. Count your steps. Say a prayer with each rep. Let your movement become a mental anchor.

- Drill 9: The Clarity Question

Pause mid-day and ask: "What matters most right now?" Write down your answer and realign your next action with it.

- Drill 10: The Silence Challenge

Turn off the radio, podcasts, and background noise on your commute or during lunch. Let silence bring clarity. What thoughts rise up when the volume is off?

HALFTIME

7

THE PIVOT ROUTINE

Post-Op Doctor's Note:

Anthony returns today. He is 5 weeks out. Shows a granulating wound at the great toe. His 2nd toe is healed. No signs of deep infection are present. X-rays today show consolidating P1 fracture on the great toe. The distal phalanx is very comminuted, and it appears that the bones are not consolidating completely. We removed the pins today. See him back in 10 days. No additional X-rays needed. At that point, we will likely let him begin working on some therapy.

"MOTIVATION IS WHAT GETS YOU STARTED. HABIT IS WHAT KEEPS YOU GOING."
— ATTRIBUTED TO JIM RYUN,
OLYMPIC TRACK & FIELD ATHLETE

Look at you—still here and still pivoting!

You didn't just skim the surface—you showed up. You leaned in, took notes, paused to reflect, and let the message meet you right where you are. Now that you understand The PIVOT Principle, something inside is shifting. I can feel it. You're not just hoping things will change—you're starting to believe you have the power to help create that change.

That, my friend, is a pivot.

This isn't the end of the book—it's the heartbeat in the middle. The part where clarity deepens, mindset sharpens, and you begin to embody what you've been learning. You're not just reading about transformation anymore. You're becoming it.

So, take a breath. Celebrate your progress.

And then let's keep going.

Because more than anything—you stayed in the game. You kept reading even when the chapters hit close to home. You paused. You questioned. You wrestled with the truth.

Maybe you even cried a little (me too).

And now? You're standing here—not just with more knowledge, but with a strategy, a rhythm, and a renewed sense of purpose.

This is your halftime reset. And we're about to level up.

Halftime Pep Talk

Hey, you.

Yes, you.

You've made it to halftime—and that's not small. That's huge. Because let's be honest: most people don't get this far. They start strong and fall off. They get inspired, but not intentional. But not you.

You've shown up. You've prayed. You've paused. You've visualized. You've offered. You've trained. You've sweated through the stretch and breathed through the burnout. And now, here you are—mid-game, mid-shift, mid-story.

And I just want to say: I see you.

I'm proud of you.

And we're not done.

See, halftime is that sacred moment in the game when everything can change. It's where champions reset. It's where the strategy gets refined. It's where the coach calls the team in, wipes off the sweat, and says:

"Now is the time to dig deeper. Now is when it counts."

So let me be that voice in your locker room today.

Let me remind you of what's already true:

- *You were built for the second half.*
- *You are stronger than the setback.*
- *You don't need perfect—you need purpose.*
- *What God started in you He will finish.*

Your PIVOT isn't just a principle. It's a pattern of perseverance. It's what turns pressure into purpose and fatigue into fuel. It's what reminds you: even in chaos, I've trained for this.

So, as you step back out on the court—into your job, your family, your future—I want you to go all in.

Play with heart.

Move with intention.

Speak life.

Stay rooted.

Keep showing up.

This isn't just the second half of the book.

This is the second wind in your journey.

Now lace up.

Refocus.

Hydrate your spirit.

And get back in the game.

Because your win is still unfolding.

And it's going to be worth it.

Second Half

8

MAKING IT PERSONAL

Y ou made it.

Not to the end—but to the *middle*. The part where it all starts to click and become yours.

By now, you've learned the foundation of *The PIVOT Principle*. Not as a theory, but as a life-tested routine—one that was born not in a boardroom or on a vision board, but in the trenches of one of the hardest, most faith-stretching seasons of my life. It was how I kept going when everything felt like it was falling apart. It helped me show up for my son, lead in my career, and hold on to a sense of purpose when my world got flipped upside down. And eventually, it became our strategy—not just to survive, but to *thrive*.

The PIVOT Principle is what steadies you when life throws you the ball with two seconds on the clock and the game is on the line. It's the move that changes everything.

And here's the beautiful part: what started as survival became transformation.

Let's take a quick time-out to recap what you've just learned—because this isn't just a list of habits. It's your *daily playbook for peace, progress, and purpose.*

Time-out: The Recap

Pray — Secure Your Foundation

Prayer is where it all begins. It's not just spiritual—it's strategic. It's the pivot foot that anchors you when life tries to spin you out of control. In prayer, you stop striving and start aligning—with God, with truth, and with what really matters.

Investigate — Stay Curious, Keep Learning

Curiosity keeps you sharp. Whether you spend five minutes reading a devotional or fifty diving into research, this habit fuels your ability to make *informed* pivots—not reactive ones. Because the smartest moves come from a place of clarity, not chaos.

Visualize — See It Before You Step Into It

Before champions take the shot, they've already taken it in their minds. Visualization trains your spirit to expect good, to imagine restoration, and to picture breakthroughs. It helps your heart believe what your eyes can't yet see.

Offer One Thing — Release What's Holding You Back

Every pivot costs something. But here's the truth: *what you're willing to release today is often the very thing that makes room for your tomorrow.* Maybe it's a bad habit. Maybe it's the pressure to please everyone. Letting go is part of leveling up.

Train — Build the Muscle Memory—Physically AND Mentally

This is where intention meets action. Whether it's walking five minutes a day, journaling through your thoughts, or practicing stillness, training is your way of saying: *I'm preparing for what I prayed for.* Faith isn't passive. It's practice.

...

This routine isn't a checklist—it's a rhythm. It's a new way of showing up to your life on purpose. Because transformation doesn't happen in big, flashy moments. It happens in the *daily* ones. The decisions no one else sees. The ones you make in quiet rooms and early mornings. And you don't need perfection to see the results. You just need *repetition.*

Making It Personal

Now that you know the *what* and the *why*, let's talk about the *how.*

Because I know life is full. You've got responsibilities, to-do lists, people to care for, and dreams you're still trying to squeeze in between emails and errands. And maybe, just maybe, you're wondering:

"How do I actually *live this out* in real life?"

Great question. You're not alone—and you're not behind. That's what this next section is all about. Together, we're going to break this down and get practical. You'll hear the most common questions I get from people just like you—real women (and some amazing men) navigating real life with real responsibilities who are ready to pivot with purpose.

So, take a deep breath.

Shake off the guilt.

And let's figure this out together. Because the second half?

That's where the game gets good.

What You're Probably Wondering...

Now, let's take a deep breath. Let go of the guilt or anxiety you may be feeling right now. And let's figure this out together. Here are some of the most common questions I get from people whom I've coached about how to actually apply all five steps of a daily PIVOT Routine into their lives.

- "What if I don't have even 25 minutes for myself each morning? Can the PIVOT Routine still work for me?"

  Spoiler alert: Yes! Start with what you have. Even five focused minutes in each area can make a difference. This routine is flexible, not rigid—it's about consistency, not perfection.

- "Do I have to do the steps in the same order every day?"

  Nope. While there's power in the flow I suggest (Pray, Investigate, Visualize, Offer, Train), life happens. Some mornings your 'Train' might come first with a walk or yoga, and other days you may need to 'Offer One Thing' before you even get out of bed. The important thing is that each piece gets attention, not that it follows a strict sequence.

- "What if I miss a day—or a whole week?"

  Grace over guilt. This is a routine, not a punishment. Think like an athlete after a missed practice: do they quit the team? Nope. They get back on the court. The win comes from returning to the habit of not beating yourself up for missing it.

- "I'm not really spiritual... is prayer still for me?"

  The 'Pray' step is about anchoring yourself. If traditional prayer doesn't resonate with you, think of this time as meditation, reflection, or intentional gratitude. The point is to ground yourself in something bigger than the chaos of your to-do list.

- "How do I know what my 'One Thing' to offer should be each day?"

  Great question. Remember to go back to the prompts I left in that chapter for you. Start by asking: What's distracting me? What's draining my focus? What's keeping me from being fully present today? The 'One Thing' might be time on social media, overcommitting to meetings, a toxic mindset, or even the need to control every detail. This offering is your sacrifice to clear the path.

- "How do I stay motivated when the results aren't showing up right away?"

  Focus on the reps, not the results. Just like weightlifting or shooting free throws, growth comes in the practice long before the scoreboard shows the win. Track your effort, not just the outcome. Remember: transformation happens quietly before it happens publicly.

- "Can I use the PIVOT Routine for a specific goal, like weight loss, job searching, or healing from heartbreak?"

  Absolutely. The PIVOT Routine is your playbook— whether you're pivoting from loss, chasing a new dream, or just needing to feel like yourself again. The daily habits remain the same; the focus of your visualization and inquiry simply adjusts to your goal.

- "What if my family or job schedule makes it impossible to have 'quiet time'?"

  Been there, sister. Do what you can, where you can. Your car can become your prayer closet. Your walk can become your training time. The shower can be your visualization space. The beauty of the PIVOT Routine is that it meets you where you are.

- "How long before I really start to feel a shift?"

  This will vary for everyone. Some feel lighter within the first week because of the intentional focus alone. Others notice mindset shifts after a few weeks. The key is to commit long enough to let the routine do its work. Small daily changes compound into big life shifts.

What Comes Next?

What comes next isn't about getting it *perfect*—it's about getting it going.

One pivot.

One pause.

One prayer.

And just like that, something starts to shift. Your thoughts begin to align with your truth. Your language reflects your hope. Your habits catch up with your purpose.

So, what will your next pivot look like?

- Will you reclaim your mornings?
- Will you choose presence over pressure?
- Will you finally give yourself permission to dream again?

Wherever you begin, just know this: you're not starting from scratch—you're starting from strength. You've built a foundation. Now it's time to apply it.

In the next few chapters, we're going to take this routine and run it through real life—your work, your relationships, your goals, and even your hard seasons.

Because this isn't just a mindset—it's a movement.

Let's keep going.

ATHLETE
Spotlight

🎾 Serena Williams
A Masterclass Athlete on PIVOT

Serena Williams isn't just one of the greatest tennis players of all time—she's a masterclass in how to work with discipline, emotional intelligence, and faith.

Here's how she models the PIVOT Principle in action:

Prayer (P): Serena has always been vocal about her faith. Before matches, in interviews, and in her personal life, she often speaks about the power of prayer and staying spiritually grounded.

Investigation (I): Serena studies her opponents relentlessly and is known for adapting her play style over decades. She learns, adjusts, and stays curious—not just about the game, but about her growth.

Visualization (V): Before every match, Serena visualizes winning. She's talked openly about seeing herself succeed—before she steps on the court.

Offering (O): She's sacrificed ego and expectations repeatedly— coming back from injuries, setbacks, even motherhood. Instead of controlling every outcome, she lets go and leans into resilience.

Training (T): No one questions her work ethic. Serena trains not just physically, but emotionally and mentally. She's navigated press conferences with grace, losses with maturity, and wins with humility.

APPLYING THE PIVOT TO WORK

Post-Op Doctor's Note:

Anthony returns today for wound assessment. 17 years old. He is about 6 weeks out from surgery. Applied new dressing today. He can now fully shower. I want him to still do dressing changes. He can begin to put a little bit of weight through the midfoot and even to the forefoot a little bit. I will see him back in 2 weeks. No X-rays needed.

"YOU DIDN'T WAKE UP TO BE MEDIOCRE."
—ROBIN ARZON, PELOTON INSTRUCTOR & VICE PRESIDENT OF FITNESS PROGRAM

Let's be real—work takes up most of our waking hours. Yet for many of us, it's the place where our routines fall apart the fastest.

How many times have you started the day with a plan—coffee in hand, to-do list ready, good intentions locked in—only to find yourself reacting to meetings, fires, and inbox overload? Before lunch, your energy is already drained, and your purpose? Completely buried under performance pressure.

That's why *The PIVOT Principle* isn't just a personal growth tool—it's a **professional game-changer**.

This chapter is about taking the habits you've built and applying them where you spend the bulk of your time: your job. Whether you work in a corner office, from your kitchen table, in the classroom, or on a job site, the PIVOT Routine helps you shift from reactive to intentional, from burnout to balance, from just checking boxes to leading with clarity.

Because when we learn to PIVOT at work, we don't just become better employees or leaders—we become better stewards of our calling.

Why Work Deserves Your PIVOT

I've been in Human Resources for over a decade, across industries like higher education, transportation, finance, and professional sports. And while employment laws stayed mostly the same, *everything else didn't*.

When I started my role in professional sports, I expected long hours—but what I didn't expect were the curveballs. What I call the "head fakes." The things you can't always plan for but have to adjust to—fast.

My first season in the NBA was... humbling. I was constantly reacting—learning every nuance, trying to prove

I could handle the pace. I was exhausted, but I paid attention. I asked questions. I worked long hours and stayed curious.

And just when I thought I had a handle on it, 2020 hit. The pandemic sent us all home "for two weeks." We all know how that turned out.

Everything shifted—how we worked, how we connected, how we measured success. And somewhere in all of that, *I changed, too.* Working remotely gave me the space to reflect. I stopped asking, "Am I doing enough?" and started asking, "Am I leading with intention?" I began to realize the PIVOT Routine wasn't just helping me survive— it was shaping how I showed up as a leader: less reactive, more reflective.

That's when I knew: this wasn't just a personal routine—it was a leadership rhythm.

Before we go further, let's take a moment to reflect on what you've read so far. Go ahead, grab that pen.

I have often heard the saying: *How you show up to work is often how you show up in life.*

What is your current relationship with your work? (Is it something you enjoy? Tolerate? Feel stuck? Feel called to do?)

____

____

____

____

____

In what ways does your work—whether you work at home, work in an office, travel for work, or however you work—in what ways does your work reflect your values? Or does it challenge them?

____

____

____

____

____

What's *one* shift you *know* you need to make, but haven't had the time or courage to do it yet?

____

____

____

This isn't about judgment. It's about *awareness*—the kind that creates space for change.

Because you weren't created to just clock in and check out.

Your work is a place where your purpose can shine—if you learn how to bring your whole self to it.

So, take a breath. Let's keep going.

Applying the PIVOT Routine at Work

Let's talk about where we spend a major portion of our energy each week—**work**. Whether you're in an office, logging in from home, running a business, or clocking in for a shift, the workplace is often the first place our routines get tested. Even with the best intentions—your morning PIVOT complete, your prayer said, your vision clear—it doesn't take long for the day to start piling on.

The calendar fills.

The emails flood in.

The pressure rises.

That's why *The PIVOT Principle* isn't just a personal growth routine—it's a professional lifeline.

This chapter is about taking the PIVOT off the page and into your workplace. Because when we learn to PIVOT at work, we don't just get more done—we protect our peace, align with our purpose, and tap into our full potential.

Whether you're leading a team or leading yourself, working for someone else or building your own vision, you are a professional. And professionals who know how to manage their mindset on the job? They gain an edge that strategy alone can't provide.

Here's how applying a PIVOT to your workday looks in real time:

P – Pray

Start your workday with intention. Before opening your inbox or walking into a meeting, pause. Whisper a prayer for wisdom, grace, and discernment. Invite God into your agenda, your conversations, and your challenges. This grounds you in purpose—not just productivity.

I – Investigate

Pay attention to what's really going on. Are you reacting from stress or responding with strategy? Take a moment to assess your energy, your emotions, and your environment. Notice the dynamics in the room, the tone in that email, the weight behind your frustration. Investigation is your superpower for staying aware and aligned.

V – Visualize

See the win before the meeting starts. Picture a conversation going well. Imagine yourself leading with clarity, not chaos. Visualization at work isn't about pretending—it's about preparing your mind to lead from a place of confidence and focus.

O – Offer

Be generous with your presence. That might mean offering encouragement to a coworker who's under pressure, showing patience in a heated moment, or lending your skills to support a team goal. This is how you build trust and influence: by giving more than what's required, from a place of overflow.

T – Train

Practice what centers you. In moments of stress, draw on the tools that help you reset: breathing deeply before a big decision, reviewing your calendar with curiosity instead of judgment, or setting a boundary that protects your peace. You don't train for game day in the middle of the game— you train daily so you can respond with skill when it counts.

This isn't about perfection. It's about presence.

The more you practice the PIVOT at work, the more you'll notice your reactions softening, your leadership sharpening, and your peace expanding—even when the pressure is on.

P is for PRAY: Inviting God Into Your Workday

Let's be honest—most of us don't forget to *show up* for work. But how often do we forget to *invite God* into it?

Prayer isn't just something you do before breakfast or on Sunday mornings. It's a sacred strategy—a leadership tool that helps you center, align, and lead with clarity throughout the day. And at work, that kind of alignment matters.

Before you respond to a sharp email, PRAY.

Before you walk into that performance review, PRAY.

Before you present your ideas, sign that contract, or even check your to-do list, PRAY.

Because prayer shifts your posture.

It reminds you: **You're not walking in alone.**

At work, it's easy to slip into survival mode—checking boxes, chasing deadlines, or fighting for a seat at the table. But prayer pulls you back to purpose. It slows your thoughts. It steadies your emotions. It helps you discern when to speak, when to wait, and when to release what you can't control.

And let's clear this up—praying at work doesn't have to be loud, long, or visible to anyone else. You can:

- **Whisper a sentence as you walk into a meeting.**

  "Lord, help me speak with wisdom and listen with grace." I've said this walking into difficult team conversations where tension was high, and it reset my heart before I even opened my mouth.

- **Pause in your car before heading inside.**

  "God, I give You this day—cover my efforts and calm my spirit." On days when I anticipated back-to-back meetings or conflict, this moment of stillness was more effective than any coffee.

- **Breathe in God's peace between back-to-back Zoom calls.**

  One deep breath in: *"Be still and know..."* One breath out: *"...that I am God."* This helped me stay grounded when juggling multiple priorities felt overwhelming.

- **Write a Scripture in the margin of your planner or Post-it on your monitor.**

  A verse like *"Commit your work to the Lord, and your plans will be established"* (Proverbs 16:3 ESV) has been my anchor during strategic planning seasons, when the pressure to perform was high.

Prayer is the invitation that turns your daily grind into divine assignment.

It doesn't change your job title—but it changes how you show up in it.

So whether your work feels like your calling or just your current assignment, praying throughout the day keeps your spirit anchored—and your leadership aligned.

PIVOT Tie-In: The "P" in the PIVOT Principle reminds you to **pray first, not last**. It's the grounding habit that shifts your mindset from self-reliance to God-dependence. When you invite God into your workday—before the stress, the meetings, the decisions—you lead from a place of peace, not pressure. Prayer doesn't just prepare your spirit; it strengthens your leadership.

PIVOT Prompt:

What can be your go-to prayer or phrase that prepares you for a tense meeting, tough conversation, or high-stakes moment during the workday? Write it down. Keep it close. Let it lead you.

____

____

____

I + V: Investigate & Visualize—Making Thoughtful Decisions at Work

Work brings choices—some small, others career-defining. From how you respond to a colleague's comment to whether you accept a new opportunity, decisions shape your professional trajectory. But when we move too fast—reacting instead of reflecting—we often regret the outcome.

That's where Investigation and Visualization come in.

Together, they help you slow down and _lead with intention_, not emotion.

Investigate is the pause. It's the quiet moment where you ask, "What's really driving my response?"

Visualize is the preparation. It's where you see the outcome before it happens—and align your actions accordingly.

Here's how to use them in real time:
- Ask, "Am I making this decision out of fear or confidence?"

Before saying yes to a project or speaking up in a meeting, notice your motive. Are you trying to prove something—or serve something bigger than yourself?

- Pause and picture success.

  Before a difficult conversation, visualize it going well. Imagine yourself speaking with calm, clarity, and compassion. This mental rehearsal creates a roadmap for your body and brain to follow.

- Check for alignment.

  Ask, "What result am I really hoping for—and is this next step moving me toward that?" Whether you're replying to an email or proposing a strategy, clarity beats urgency every time.

PIVOT Tie-In: These are the "I" and "V" of the PIVOT Principle. Together, they remind you to stay connected to the bigger picture—so you're not just reacting or checking boxes, but choosing actions that reflect your purpose and priorities.

PIVOT Prompt:

Think of a decision you're currently facing at work.

____

____

____

What emotions are influencing it?

____

____

____

What outcome do you *truly* want—and what would it look like to respond from a place of clarity instead of fear?

____

____

____

____

Offer: Releasing the Workday Weight

Work can come with a lot of hidden weight—unspoken expectations, relentless deadlines, subtle comparisons, and internal pressure to perform. Some of that pressure is external. But much of it? We carry ourselves.

Every day, you have a choice: **Will you carry the weight—or will you offer it?**

Offering doesn't mean giving up. It means **letting go of what's not yours to hold**, so you can focus your energy where it counts most.

At work, your offering might look like:

- **Turning your phone on Do Not Disturb to reclaim your focus.**

  When distractions mount, protecting your mental space is a gift to both your peace and your productivity.

- **Saying no to a last-minute request that would cost you peace or performance.**

  Setting a boundary isn't selfish—it's wise stewardship of your energy and priorities.

- **Logging off on time—without guilt.**

   Rest is not a reward. It's part of your rhythm. And offering the rest of your day back to God is an act of trust that what's undone can wait—or wasn't meant for you to carry in the first place.

Offering is about surrender. It's choosing to release what's heavy so you can remain present, aligned, and whole.

PIVOT Tie-In: The "O" in the PIVOT Principle invites you to let go of anything that pulls you off course—so you can stay grounded in what matters most. It's the step that makes room for margin, peace, and divine partnership in your work.

PIVOT Prompt:

What's one thing you've been carrying at work—mentally, emotionally, or physically—that you know it's time to release?

____

____

____

What would it look like to offer it back to God and trust that He's still in control, even if you set it down?

____

____

____

T is for TRAIN: Emotional Awareness at Work

You don't have to be the boss to lead with emotional intelligence. You just have to be aware.

Work environments are full of pressure points—conflict, urgency, shifting expectations, surprise feedback, and miscommunication. Without emotional awareness, it's easy to get swept up in reaction mode. But training your mind helps you respond with wisdom instead of impulse.

And just like any form of training, this takes practice.

At work, training might look like:

- **Taking three deep breaths before responding to a frustrating email.**

  It gives your nervous system a moment to reset so you don't hit "send" in a moment of tension you'll later regret.

- **Choosing curiosity over criticism in a tense conversation.**

  Asking *"Help me understand what led to this?"* instead of assuming intent can de-escalate conflict and build bridges in a culture that often reacts with blame.

- **Noticing when you're overstimulated and stepping away for a short break.**

  A two-minute reset—whether it's prayer, a walk, or silence—can do more for your productivity than pushing through in a state of stress.

PIVOT Tie-In: This is the "T" in the PIVOT Principle: training your mind to *respond* rather than *react*. Emotional maturity isn't reserved for leaders with titles—it's a daily decision for anyone who wants to be respected, resilient, and clear under pressure.

PIVOT Prompt:

What's one situation at work where you tend to react quickly—maybe out of frustration, insecurity, or urgency?

____

____

____

What would it look like to pause, train your response, and show up with emotional clarity instead?

____

____

____

Real Talk: Professionals Who Pivot

You don't have to be in the C-suite to lead your life with excellence. When you apply the PIVOT Routine at work, you:

- Set the tone for your own productivity.
- Protect your emotional bandwidth.
- Align your output with your values.

And if you *do* lead others—whether it's a team, a classroom, a family, or a client base—we'll go deeper into the next section to show how to apply the PIVOT specifically to leadership.

But for now, just know this:

Every professional needs a way to reset. To refocus. To stay grounded in the middle of pressure.

That's what the PIVOT Routine gives you.

And it's already in your hands.

...

Before we move into how leaders can model *The PIVOT Principle* in more formal leadership roles, let's take a breath and reflect on how you can start applying *The PIVOT Principle* and Routine to your everyday work. Grab your pen!

Where in your workday do you feel most aligned—and where do you feel off-center?

____

____

____

____

What part of your PIVOT Routine feels hardest to apply during the workweek? Why might that be?

____

____

____

____

What boundary—physical, emotional, or spiritual— would help you bring your best to work?

____

____

____

____

What's one professional or workday habit you'd like to train or strengthen over the next 30 days?

____

____

____

How can you incorporate prayer, reflection, or visualization before your meetings, errands, or other tasks during the workday?

____

____

____

Now that you've taken a moment to reflect on how *The PIVOT Principle* and a daily PIVOT Routine can support your personal work rhythm, let's take it one step further.

Because if you *are* in a position of leadership (or maybe you want to be in a position of leadership)—whether you manage a team, run a business, mentor others, or simply influence the culture around you—how you PIVOT doesn't just impact your day... it impacts everyone connected to you.

Let's talk about what it looks like when *leaders* pivot with purpose.

When Leaders PIVOT First

Leadership is not about doing *more*—it's about doing *what matters most* with intention and integrity. And when your calendar is packed, your inbox overflowing, and your team depending on you, a daily PIVOT routine becomes your secret weapon.

Let's break down how leaders can lead well, stay focused, and build trust by using the PIVOT every single day.

Leaders Seek Prayer as Strategy

Now, I know the moment we bring up "prayer," some leaders might feel a little tension. Maybe you wouldn't call yourself a "prayer warrior." Maybe your leadership style leans more into data, strategy, or vision boards than devotionals. But hear me out.

In today's world—where change is constant, pressure is high, and clarity can feel hard to come by—*every leader needs a North Star*. You need more than a to-do list or a calendar. You need divine direction. You need a way to lead that's grounded, centered, and wise. And that's what prayer does.

Prayer isn't just for the spiritually elite—it's for the emotionally mature. It's how strong leaders stay steady. It's how wise leaders make decisions. It's how courageous leaders take bold steps—without carrying the full weight alone.

Prayer is not about getting everything right. It's about getting aligned.

Because let's be real—in the 21st century, with everything we're carrying (global uncertainty, staff burnout, economic shifts, Diversity Equity Inclusion (DEI) fatigue, cultural polarization—and that's just on Mondays!), we need more than leadership hacks. We need *holy habits.*

And there's no better leadership model than the One who led with both compassion and conviction—Jesus. He paused. He prayed. He prioritized His connection with God before making decisions, healing the masses, or confronting opposition.

If *He* needed that kind of alignment, so do we.

Since we're talking about prayer and leadership, let's zoom in on someone who modeled this rhythm with power and purpose—straight from the pages of Scripture: **Nehemiah.**

Nehemiah wasn't a priest or a prophet. He was a high-performing, marketplace professional—a cupbearer to the king. And when he learned that the walls of Jerusalem were in ruins, he didn't rush into action. He didn't gather a team or make a strategic plan.

He *prayed first*.

"When I heard these things, I sat down and wept. For some days I mourned and fasted and prayed before the God of heaven."

— Nehemiah 1:4

His leadership began on his knees. And later, when the king asked what he wanted, Nehemiah didn't respond with a rehearsed elevator pitch—he *prayed again* in real time:

"Then I prayed to the God of heaven, and I answered the king..."

— Nehemiah 2:4–5

Nehemiah reminds us that strong leaders don't always have immediate answers—but they do have *immediate access* to the Source of wisdom.

Whew. What I wouldn't give for more leaders in the HR space—heck, in *any* space—who pause to pray before making the big decisions!

So, let's bring prayer application to the present day. What does a prayer-led leader look like in real time?

Start your leadership day with:

- A prayer for discernment before major meetings or presentations
- Covering your team by name, asking God to strengthen and guide them
- Confessing your limitations and inviting God to lead through you

Prayer is your leadership *posture*—before it ever becomes your platform.

And don't forget: Jesus Himself often withdrew to pray before teaching, healing, or facing hard conversations. *If He needed that pause, that clarity, that connection—so do we.*

Now, as you're pondering the place of prayer in your daily PIVOT as a leader, let's take a few minutes—yes, even in the middle of your daily hustle—to pause and reflect. These questions aren't about getting it right. They're about getting real, particularly with what kind of leader YOU want to be. As always... grab a pen.

What's one area of leadership where you've been trying to figure it out all on your own? Managing your household or family? Problem employee? Team growth?

When was the last time you paused to pray before making a tough decision—or sending that email—or calling that meeting?

Who on your team, or in your household, or on your committee, needs prayer?

Wrapping It Up: Your Work, Your Leadership, Your PIVOT

By now, you can probably see it: the PIVOT Routine isn't just personal practice—it's a professional power move. It's how you stop letting your day lead you and start leading your day with clarity, conviction, and peace.

Whether you're clocking in from your kitchen, leading a team across multiple time zones, managing clients, or managing chaos—this routine gives you a framework. Not for perfection, but for purpose.

When you *pray*, you ground yourself in wisdom, not just willpower.

When you *investigate*, you stay curious and sharp—learning instead of just reacting.

When you *visualize*, you begin to see beyond your current circumstance.

When you *offer one thing*, you lead with focus instead of frenzy.

And when you *train*, you build the consistency needed to sustain the impact you're here to make.

Leaders, professionals, changemakers—this is your moment to reset how you show up.

Because the truth is, your leadership isn't just about results. It's about rhythm. It's not just about output. It's about overflowing.

From the break room to the boardroom, your PIVOT matters.

So tomorrow when the emails flood in, the tension rises, or the schedule shifts unexpectedly—remember, you've got a new routine. You've got a way back to clarity. You've got a rhythm that works.

Let's keep building it—together.

Journal Prompts for Applying the PIVOT to Your Work

Take 5–10 minutes to reflect on these questions as you prepare to bring your PIVOT Routine into your workplace. Don't overthink it—just write what comes up.

1. Where in your workday do you feel the most overwhelmed or distracted? How could a daily PIVOT routine bring more clarity or peace to that area?

2. What does "success" look like for you at work—beyond your job title or performance review? What does it feel like?

3. How often do you pause and pray before responding to an email, making a decision, or entering a difficult conversation? What might change if you did?

4. What is one small skill, piece of knowledge, or area of your industry you want to explore this week? How can you intentionally "investigate" to grow your expertise?

5. When the day gets busy or stressful, what are your go-to distractions or excuses? What is one "offering" you're willing to give up today to stay focused and present?

6. Visualize yourself at the end of today. What's the ONE thing you want to feel proud of when you close your laptop or leave the office?

7. What are some ways you can "train" your mind at work—whether through leadership development,

mindfulness, or intentional learning? How will you commit to this daily?

8. If you led your team or workday with the PIVOT Principle at the center, what would look different? How would your coworkers, clients, or partners experience you?

The PIVOT Workplace Challenge

What if your team didn't just survive the workday—but truly thrived through it?

This **Workplace Challenge** is your opportunity to apply *The PIVOT Principle* in real-time, with real people, right where you work. Whether you're in a cubicle, a conference room, or on a Zoom screen, the PIVOT Routine can be the catalyst for more intentional leadership, clearer communication, and greater workplace well-being.

Here's how to get started:

Step 1: Form a "PIVOT Circle"

Gather 3–8 coworkers, team members, or colleagues who are interested in personal and professional growth. You can meet in person, online, or during lunch breaks.

Bonus idea: Include someone from a different department or role. Cross-pollination leads to fresh insights.

Step 2: Choose a Weekly Rhythm

Pick a consistent day and time to meet (30–45 minutes/ week works great). Over 6–8 weeks, walk through the book together—one habit at a time.

Suggested Flow:

- Week 1: Introduction + Pre-Game Assessment
- Week 2: Pray
- Week 3: Investigate
- Week 4: Visualize
- Week 5: Offer One Thing
- Week 6: Train

- Week 7: Work + Leadership Focus
- Week 8: Celebrate + Share Growth

Step 3: Make It Personal

During each session:

- Share one insight or takeaway.
- Discuss how you applied (or plan to apply) the habit at work.
- End with one action step or journal prompt for the week.

Optional Challenge Elements

- Mindful Mondays: Start each week with 5 minutes of silence or breathwork as a group.
- 'One Thing' Check-Ins: Encourage team members to text or Slack one 'thing' they're offering up that day.
- Victory Wall: Create a shared space (physical or virtual) to post progress, wins, or pivots worth celebrating.

10

APPLYING THE PIVOT
TO RELATIONSHIPS

Post-Op Doctor's Note:

11/21/2018 - Anthony returns today. He is a pleasant 17-year-old who sustained a lawnmower injury to his right toe and 2nd toe. He says he has not had any pain. He has been walking with his boot as tolerated, putting almost his full weight on it without having any significant difficulty. He denies any calf pain. Has not had any numbness or tingling in his lower extremities. Only 8 weeks out and he says this is feeling like a normal toe, and he is relatively well and happy.

Physical Examination:

Well-nourished male who is alert and oriented x3. He has a pleasant affect, well cooperative with exam, laying comfortably on the examination table in no acute distress. Examination of the patient's right foot, his 2nd toe is completely healed. No signs of infection. Really looks great from his amputation. Has a regular rate and intact sensation of his distal extremity to light touch. Calf is soft and non-tender. No signs of DVT.

"THE MOST HARMONIOUS COUPLES ARE THE ONES
WHO LEARN TO PLAY ON THE SAME TEAM."
— ARTHUR C. BROOKS, HARVARD PROFESSOR

Let's be honest—relationships are where real work happens.

It's one thing to practice the PIVOT routine alone in the quiet of your home office. It's another thing entirely to remember your PIVOT when your teenager is rolling their eyes, your coworker misses a deadline, your spouse is distant, or your friend's words hit deeper than they know. Remember, when I started writing about *The PIVOT Principle,* I had a teenager at home who had just lost his dream and a husband who blamed himself. I wanted to talk it out, while the two men in the house simply wanted to forget about what happened and do anything BUT talk.

But if *The PIVOT Principle* has taught me anything, it's this: how we show up in our relationships matters just as much as how we show up in our goals, our careers, or our personal growth. Because no matter how disciplined our morning routine is, how successful your career becomes, or how strong your prayer life may be—if your relationships are misaligned, that imbalance will eventually affect every other area of your life. The peace you're building within should be reflected in how you love, listen, lead, and support others. Your pivot isn't just personal—it's relational.

Healthy, life-giving relationships don't happen by accident.

They are built—deliberately, patiently, and prayerfully. They require intention when it would be easier to withdraw. They require grace when someone disappoints us. And they require a willingness to pause long enough to ask a hard but holy question: *What direction do I need to turn right now to protect this connection?*

This isn't about avoiding conflict or sugarcoating hard truths. It's about aligning your heart with God's heart before you engage. It's about responding, not reacting. And it's about knowing that relationships thrive not on perfection, but on consistent, Spirit-led effort.

Remember this: Every strong team needs a playbook.

This chapter is yours—for showing up in relationships with grace, strategy, and God-led intention. Think of it as your training ground for love that listens, peace that persists, and boundaries that bless. Because how you show up in your relationships will either multiply your growth— or silently sabotage it.

Why Relationships Deserve Your PIVOT

One of the most powerful things you can do during your PIVOT routine—especially when it comes to relationships— is to *pray for your people*, starting with the one closest to you: your spouse.

I'll be honest with you. Andre and I have been married for 13 years, and even though we love each other deeply, we've had our fair share of silent standoffs and differing opinions on everything from parenting to priorities. Both of us came into this marriage as independent, purpose-driven professionals. That kind of strength is beautiful—but it also means we've had to learn how to lead *together* instead of in parallel.

And let me tell you—prayer has saved us more times than I can count.

Not the "Lord, please fix him" kind of prayer. (Though I've definitely prayed that before!) I'm talking about the kind of prayer that invites God to change me first. The kind that calms my emotions long enough for me to remember who Andre really is—his heart, his intentions, his integrity. The kind that helps me stop assuming the worst and start anchoring myself in what I *know* to be true: that we want the same things... we just sometimes have a different way of going about getting them.

There are some bonus perks that come with making prayer for your spouse a regular part of your morning PIVOT Routine:

- Clarity over confusion: Prayer has a way of quieting all the noise. It helps you sort through the feelings and see the facts—what's really going on versus what's just emotional static.
- Softened hearts: Even when there's distance, prayer invites God into the space between you. And where He is, bitterness can't thrive. Pride starts to melt. Compassion shows up.

- Spiritual alignment: When you consistently pray for your spouse, you begin to align with God's vision for your relationship—not just your own preferences. You start moving as a team again.

- Fresh perspective: Prayer shifts the focus from *what's not working* to *what's worth fighting for.* And when you remember what you're building together, you show up with more grace, more patience, and more hope.

So, if there's tension in your marriage—or even if there's not—let prayer be your first move, not your last resort. You'd be surprised how many "hard conversations" get easier when your heart is already aligned with Heaven.

Scriptures for Relationship Alignment

When emotions run high, silence feels heavy, or connection feels strained, the Word can offer the wisdom, grounding, and grace you need to PIVOT well in your relationship. Here are a few scriptures I turn to when I need to realign my heart before reacting:

- Ephesians 4:2-3

    "Be completely humble and gentle; be patient, bearing with one another in love. Make every effort to keep the unity of the Spirit through the bond of peace."

    → Use this verse to pray for unity and humility when tensions rise.

- Colossians 3:13-14

    "Bear with each other and forgive one another if any of you has a grievance against someone. Forgive as

the Lord forgave you. And over all these virtues put on love, which binds them all together in perfect unity."

→ Perfect for those moments when forgiveness feels hard but necessary.

- Proverbs 15:1 (NLT)

"A gentle answer deflects anger, but harsh words make tempers flare."

→ A go-to reminder for choosing softness over sarcasm in communication.

- 1 Peter 3:7 (NLT)

"In the same way, you husbands must give honor to your wives. Treat your wife with understanding as you live together... she is your equal partner in God's gift of new life. Treat her as you should so your prayers will not be hindered."

→ A powerful verse for spouses to remember the weight and beauty of mutual honor.

- Ecclesiastes 4:9-10

"Two are better than one... If either of them falls down, one can help the other up."

→ Use this to center your heart in gratitude for the partnership God has given you—even when it feels challenging.

→ Use any or all these scriptures to meditate on during your prayer time, too.

The PIVOT Principle for Relationship Growth

Let's walk through what it looks like to apply each part of the PIVOT routine to your relationships. Because growth in relationships doesn't happen overnight—and it certainly doesn't happen by accident. It happens when we make a daily decision to love well, speak wisely, and lead with emotional maturity.

This framework isn't just theory—it's a rhythm you can lean into every single day, especially when things feel off or uncertain.

P — Prayer for Your People

Start with prayer. Before you plan what you're going to say or strategize how you'll respond, *pray first.* Prayer has the power to shift your perspective before you ever speak a word. Ask God to soften your heart toward the other person. Ask Him to help you listen without defensiveness. And most importantly, pray for *them*—not just that they would change, but that they would be covered in peace, wisdom, and clarity too.

When I pray for Andre, especially when we've had a disagreement, it changes me. Not him. It reminds me that we're on the same team. It helps me release my grip on the need to be right and lean into the desire to be *close.*

I — Investigation Through Curiosity

Curiosity is your superpower in conflict. Instead of jumping to conclusions or assuming you know what they meant, take a breath and ask a better question. Don't interrogate— *investigate.* Curiosity sounds like:

"Can you help me understand what you were feeling when that happened?"

"I noticed something shifted—can we talk about it?"

Asking questions creates space. It invites vulnerability. It shifts the tone from *accusation* to *exploration.* In relationships, curiosity builds bridges that assumptions often burn.

V — Visualization of Healthy Connections

Before you go into that tough conversation—or even before you walk into the kitchen where you know tension is waiting—pause. Close your eyes for just a few seconds and *visualize* what a healthy connection with this person could look like. Not what they need to say or do—but how you want to show up.

Visualize speaking with kindness, listening with your full heart, and walking away feeling proud of how you handled it. The more you train your mind to imagine peace, the more naturally you'll begin to pursue it.

O — Offering of Ego, Control, or Being Right

Let's be honest—sometimes what blocks connection isn't what they said. It's our ego. Our need to be right. Our desire to control how someone sees us, how the conversation plays out, or how quickly it gets resolved.

In these moments, ask yourself: *What do I need to release to make space for real peace?*

Maybe it's the need to win. Maybe it's the story you're telling yourself about their motives. Whatever it is, offering it up—laying it down in humility—may be the very thing that opens the door to healing.

And here's what I've learned: letting go isn't weakness. It's spiritual maturity.

T — Training for Emotional Intelligence

Emotional intelligence isn't something you're born with— it's something you *build*. One decision at a time. When you choose to pause instead of pounce, when you reflect instead of react, when you listen longer than you speak— that's training.

And like any athlete, training requires consistency. You won't get it perfect every time. But you will get stronger. You'll notice yourself pausing more, noticing more, caring deeper, and responding better. And that's the kind of growth that blesses every relationship you have.

ATHLETE
Spotlight

🏀 Kobe Bryant – Legacy of Love and Intentional Relationships

Kobe Bryant was known worldwide for his "Mamba Mentality"–an unrelenting drive to master his craft. But what many people came to admire most in the later years of his life was how he pivoted from performer to relational leader–husband, father, mentor, and advocate.

Though Kobe's early career was marked by intense focus and personal challenges, his later years showed a powerful transformation in how he prioritized relationships–particularly with his wife, Vanessa, and their daughters. He frequently spoke about how intentional he became with time, communication, and presence once he retired from the NBA.

> "You have to dance beautifully in the box you
> are comfortable dancing in. It doesn't mean you can't expand it.
> But you have to know who you are and stay true to that."
> – Kobe Bryant

- A Husband Who Pivoted: Kobe was honest about the hard seasons in his marriage–and he worked to repair and strengthen that connection. His love for Vanessa was both private and public, shown through quiet loyalty and consistent acts of devotion.

- A Present Father: His daughter Gianna ("Gigi") wasn't just his child–she was his teammate. Their courtside moments, shared love for the game, and his role as "Girl Dad" inspired millions. He wasn't just present–he was all-in.

- A Champion for Connection: After retirement, Kobe used his platform to create stories for children, empower female athletes, and teach the next generation not just how to win–but how to live and love well.

PIVOT Connection: Kobe's evolution from lone competitor to relational leader illustrates exactly what this chapter teaches: that greatness is measured not just by what you achieve, but by how you show up in your relationships.

Micro-PIVOT Practices for Everyday Relationship Moments

We've spent a lot of time building your personal rhythm and applying *The PIVOT Principle* to your work life—but when it comes to relationships, the application often looks less like a full-blown routine and more like a series of everyday decisions.

This section won't follow the same structure as the last few. Why? Because relationships don't operate on a perfect checklist—and applying the PIVOT here isn't about managing others. It's about managing how *you* show up in moments that matter most.

You won't always have time to pause for 30 minutes of journaling when your partner, coworker, child, or best friend hits a nerve. Sometimes, all you have is 10 seconds and a choice. That's where **micro-pivots** come in.

These are the small, in-the-moment practices that can shift the temperature of a conversation, rebuild trust, and strengthen the connection—one intentional choice at a time. No big speeches. No dramatic interventions. Just honest, grace-filled actions that move your relationship forward instead of letting it spiral.

Let's walk through a few. You'll be surprised how powerful the little things can be.

- Pause and Pray before you respond to a tough comment.

You know that moment when someone says something that stings—and your first instinct is to clap back or shut down? That's the perfect place for a micro-pivot. Take a breath. Whisper a quick prayer: *"Lord, help me respond from a place of wisdom, not woundedness."*

Even just 10 seconds of silence before speaking can shift the entire tone of a conversation. Prayer invites clarity in and keeps chaos out.

- Ask a better question instead of jumping to conclusions.

Instead of assuming intent—*"They're just being difficult"*—try a question that opens the door to understanding:

"Hey, is something else going on today?"

"Can we talk through what you meant by that?"

"I'm noticing something feels off—how are you really doing?"

Better questions create better outcomes. They slow down your reactions and speed up your empathy.

- Offer reflective listening

Repeat back what you heard before offering your view. Sometimes, the greatest gift you can offer in a tense moment is simply making someone feel heard. Try saying:

"What I hear you saying is that you felt unsupported when I made that decision. Is that right?"

This isn't about agreeing with everything—it's about showing respect and clarity before moving forward. Reflective listening builds trust, even in hard conversations.

- Take a 5-minute reset when emotions are high— you'll come back with a better perspective.

When your emotions are running the show, it's almost impossible to show up with the wisdom and grace you *want* to bring. Step away. Go for a walk, splash cold water on your face, sit in the bathroom, and breathe.

This isn't avoidance—it's emotional maturity. Give your nervous system a chance to regulate before you re-engage. You'll return with calmer thoughts, clearer language, and a heart that's better aligned.

Bonus Micro-PIVOT: Choose kindness in the small moments.

Leave the note.

Send the encouraging text. Apologize first. Ask how they're doing without expecting a full answer. Sometimes the smallest kindness shifts the entire emotional temperature of a relationship.

These micro-pivots are like your relationship reps. They may not feel dramatic or impressive in the moment—but over time, they build muscle. They create a rhythm of grace, accountability, and trust. And that rhythm? That's what keeps love steady, even when life gets loud.

Before we move on, take a moment to slow down. Grab your journal, the notes app on your phone, or the back of a napkin if you have to—but don't skip this. Reflection is where the real shift begins. Because the truth is, these micro-pivots aren't just concepts to remember—they're habits to embody.

Let's make it personal:

Which micro-pivot feels hardest for you to practice—and why?

(Is it pausing before reacting? Asking better questions? Offering kindness when you're hurt?)

____

____

____

____

Think of a recent relational conflict or tension.

What would have changed if you had paused, prayed, or chosen curiosity instead of assuming?

____

____

____

____

What's one relationship in your life that needs more presence and less perfection right now?

What's a small act of connection you can offer this week?

____

____

____

____

Y'all, I just can't help it at this point in our reading. I want to pray over you right now, over your relationships, over your heartaches, over your friendships.

Father,

Thank You for the relationships You've placed in my friend's life—each one a classroom, each moment an opportunity to grow in love, patience, and understanding. Open their eyes to see beyond what's said. Open their ears to hear the needs beneath the noise. Help them pause before reacting, ask before assuming, and lean in when it feels easier to walk away.

Where there's frustration, plant peace.

Where there's pride, birth humility.

Where there's misunderstanding, let clarity rise.

Teach them to show up—present, prayerful, and full of grace—for the people You've entrusted to their care: loved ones, colleagues, friends, even those who are hard to love. Let their words be gentle, their tone be healing, and their heart be aligned with Yours.

They don't want to just manage relationships. They want to honor them.

So today, take their reactions, their assumptions, and their unmet expectations—and I ask for Your wisdom so that they may lead with love.

In Jesus' name, Amen.

Closing Thoughts: The Power of Staying Soft and Steady

There is no winning in relationships. There is only building, learning, and repairing. Soft hearts and strong boundaries are not mutually exclusive. In fact, they are the secret to healthy connections.

A pivot isn't spinning in circles. It's choosing your next step—with intention, faith, and care.

So, pivot. Pivot toward grace. Pivot toward peace. Pivot toward the relationships that matter most.

One habit. One choice. One day at a time.

Journal Prompts for Applying Your PIVOT to Relationships

You've just explored how small, intentional shifts—your micro-pivots—can make a powerful difference in your relationships. But don't just read this... *live* this. Let's take a few moments to slow down and really think through how these ideas show up in your own life.

Grab your journal, find a quiet spot, and give yourself space to process. These prompts aren't about getting the "right" answer—they're about getting real with where you are and where you want to grow.

Let's go.

P — Prayer for Your People
- Who needs your prayers today?
- What would it look like to surrender control and trust God in this relationship?

I — Investigation Through Curiosity
- When did I last listen to understand, not just reply?
- Where am I making assumptions that need to be cleared up?

V — Visualization of Healthy Connections
- What does the healthiest version of this relationship look like?
- How can I show up as that person, regardless of their response?

O — Offering of Ego, Control, or Being Right
- What am I clinging to that might be keeping us stuck?
- What would it look like to release that—today?

T — Training for Emotional Intelligence
- Which relational skill am I practicing right now?
- Who models it well, and what can I learn from them?

The PIVOT Relationship Challenge

What if small, intentional shifts could breathe new life into your most important relationships?

Over the next 7 days, choose *one relationship* to focus on—spouse, friend, sibling, coworker, or even your child. Each day, practice one micro-pivot from this chapter with that person. You don't have to announce it. Just show up with intention.

Here's how it works:
- Day 1 – Pause & Pray before responding.

- Day 2 – Ask a better question.
- Day 3 – Practice reflective listening.
- Day 4 – Take a 5-minute emotional reset before re-engaging.
- Day 5 – Offer one act of kindness or encouragement.
- Day 6 – Apologize first if needed. Don't wait to be "right."
- Day 7 – Write a short note or send a text expressing genuine appreciation.

Keep a simple journal log each day to reflect on how your words, energy, or emotions shifted. Notice how small changes impact connection, peace, and understanding.

This isn't about fixing every relationship in a week—it's about building a rhythm of presence, humility, and love.

11

ONE FINAL NOTE ON PIVOTS

Post-Op Doctor's Note:

03/05/2019 – Anthony returns today. We preserved the toe. We repaired the exterior tendon and tried to fix the bone. He is now almost 6 months out from his injury. Pain is 0/10. The toe has survived. Mild skin discoloration at the great toe, but definitely healed. Nailbed forming.

"KNOWING YOUR PURPOSE WILL HELP KEEP YOU ON TRACK AND REMIND YOU HOW TO SHOW UP.."
— APOLO ANTON OHNO, SHORT TRACK SPEED SKATER, 8X MEDALIST, WINTER OLYMPICS

Let me say this plainly: you don't need to replicate *my* PIVOT.

You need to *design your own.*

This book began with a story—a real one. A story of loss, fear, faith, and hope. And from that story came a routine. A rhythm. A lifeline. What we call *The PIVOT Principle.*

But even with all the stories, drills, and tools I've given you, there's one final truth I want you to carry with you:

The PIVOT only works when it becomes *yours*.

Maybe you started this book looking for peace.

For clarity.

For a new way forward.

Maybe life was full of transition, or you were simply tired of carrying it all without a rhythm that made sense for *you.*

Wherever you started, I want to celebrate something:

You made it.

Not just to the final chapter—but through your *own* inner game.

You showed up, you leaned in, and you kept turning the page—even when it challenged you.

Now, you know:

The PIVOT isn't just about changing direction.

It's about anchoring your life to what matters most—and learning to move with purpose.

Because no matter how strong you are... how successful... how spiritual...

Change will come again.

The question isn't *if*—it's *how* you'll respond the next time life calls for one.

And now? Now you have a plan.

Now you have a rhythm.

Now you have a *playbook.*

Don't Just Read This. Live This.

Your routine might not look like mine.

Your mornings might be louder.

Your prayers shorter.

Your offerings more complex.

Maybe you're navigating grief, raising kids, managing deadlines—or all three.

That's okay.

The goal was never to copy my path.

The goal was to find your rhythm.

To *personalize* the practice.

To lead with intention when life feels anything but predictable.

So let me remind you what this looks like—when *you* live it:

- **Pray** for peace—even when it feels like you're surrounded by chaos.
- **Investigate** what's true—not just what's loud or urgent.
- **Visualize** the life God designed for you, even when your current reality looks nothing like it.
- **Offer** up ego, fear, perfectionism, and anything else keeping you stuck.
- **Train** your body, your habits, your mind, and your hope—because discipline fuels destiny.

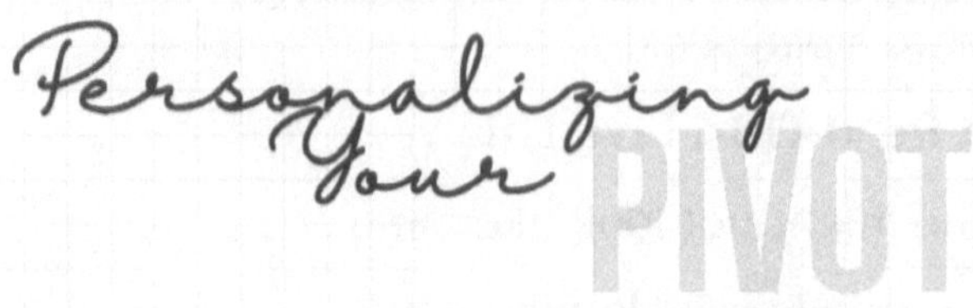

Personalizing Your PIVOT

Pray - In your words, your way. Whispered on the commute. Written in your journal.
Sung in the shower.
Don't overthink it - just connect.

Investigate - Stay curious. Whether you're googling career trends, diving into scripture, or observing what brings you peace - keep learning.

Visualize - See what's possible. Close your eyes. Picture the person you're becoming. Dream big - and then dream again.

Offer - Make space. Let go of one thing that no longer serves you so that you can move toward what will.

Train - Prepare. Work out. Transform your body, mind, and spirit for the best version of yourself. You're going to need that strength!

That's how you PIVOT with power.

Designing Your Own PIVOT

Let's bring this home.

You don't need a perfect morning routine. You need a meaningful one.

You don't need to perform—you need to *practice*. Because practice is where peace is formed. Practice is where transformation takes root.

So, ask yourself:

- What do *I* need to feel grounded before *my* day begins?
- Which PIVOT habit could serve as *my* anchor during a chaotic season?
- What are *my* non-negotiables—spiritually, mentally, emotionally?

This routine is yours now. Shape it around your life. Let it evolve as you grow.

As You Go...

As you close this book, I hope you know you're not starting over.

You're starting from wisdom.

From strategy.

From spiritual alignment.

And you are not alone. You have a God who goes before you. A community of people cheering for you. And a future that still holds promise.

Here's my prayer for you:

That you would PIVOT boldly.

That you would PIVOT honestly.

That you would PIVOT humbly.

And that every single pivot—big or small—would bring you one step closer to the life God has been preparing for you all along.

You are more ready than you know.

Peace, Love, & PIVOT.

– Dr. Shelley Kemp

The Final Buzzer—Epilogue

Post-Op Doctor's Note:

Anthony follows up today. He is 17 years old. He sustained an injury to his right foot back in September 2018 with a lawnmower. Partial amputation. **Pain is 0/10. Shows a healed wound with no signs of infection.** The hypertrophic granulation tissue that was present previously is gone. The nail on the great toe. He has really no IP flexion, but it is not very tender. **The length of the toe has been maintained. At this point, no further treatment is required.**

> "You can practice shooting eight hours a day, but if your technique is wrong, then all you become is very good at shooting the wrong way."
>
> — Michael Jordan

There's a line in the final doctor's note from Anthony's surgery that I've never forgotten:

"No further treatment is required."

At face value, it meant the physical healing was complete. But for me—for us—it means so much more. It meant: *We made it.*

Back in September 2018, when that lawnmower accident shifted our entire world, we didn't know what the future would hold. We didn't know if Anthony would walk again without pain. We didn't know if he'd ever play sports again. We didn't know how we would explain the trauma, the grief, or the faith it would take just to get through each day. But here we are—nearly seven years later. And if you've read this far, you know by now...

Everything pivoted.

Not just Anthony's foot. Not just our routines. But our expectations, our priorities, our prayers.

We thought Anthony would head off to a university, major in mechanical engineering, maybe join the military reserves for the benefits. We imagined the smooth, scripted version of success—school, degree, career, maybe some recognition along the way. But God had another plan. And honestly? So did Anthony's heart.

Yes, he went to college. But it was during the pandemic, and let's be real—it wasn't the "best years of your life" experience we'd sold him on. After a year, he made a brave decision. He pivoted. He started apprenticing as a diesel mechanic, committed himself to the trade, and earned his license.

Today, he works at one of his dream companies— Porsche—as a Bronze-level technician. (Like what

20-something-year-old young adult wouldn't want to drive around in Porsches all day "test-driving"?)

He's thriving.

He's independent.

He's thoughtful, funny, humble, and wise beyond his years.

He's healed.

And I don't just mean his foot. I mean his purpose. His path. His peace.

What we thought was the end of one dream became the beginning of a better one.

That's what this book has been about all along.

Your pivot may not come through trauma. But it will come through *truth*.

Truth about who you are. What you value. And who you're becoming.

If our family can pivot—through blood, tears, surgeries, setbacks, and complete reimagining of what the future could be—*so can you.*

No matter where life takes you next, remember:

The goal isn't to go back. It's to move forward—wiser, stronger, and anchored in grace.

There's still purpose in your pivot.

And the best part?

You're just getting started.

The End

FILM ROOM REFLECTIONS— APPENDICES

From Reading to Writing: The Power of the Pen

You've made it this far—not just through the chapters, but through the *work*. And now, it's time to make it personal.

Reading *The PIVOT Principle* was just the warm-up. The real transformation starts when you *practice* what you've learned day by day, with intention. One of the most powerful ways to do that? Journaling.

I've had seasons where I drifted. Even after learning this routine, I've skipped steps. Substituted prayer for a scroll. Ignored my body. Let my mind race. And I felt it— emotionally, physically, spiritually. The weight of life piled up. Communication in my marriage faded. I lost my rhythm.

But the beauty of the PIVOT is that it's always ready when you are. You can come back to it again and again. Not out of guilt—but because peace, purpose, and clarity live on the other side of that pause.

Now, to help you see what that looks like in real life, I'm sharing a few of my actual journal entries—unedited, honest, and written in real time. These are not polished.

Some are messy. Some are bold. Some are quiet. But all of them reflect my daily attempt to stay grounded, stay grateful, and stay growing.

There's no right way to journal. If you've ever felt like you were doing it wrong—let me be the first to say: you weren't. Just write what's real. That's how transformation begins.

So, grab your pen, your notebook, or even the back of a receipt if that's all you've got. These entries are shared not to impress you, but to *invite* you—into your own practice, your own rhythm, your own pivot.

PIVOTs in Progress: Journal Entries from Your Coach

Saturday, January 19, 2019

Proverbs 31:30 (ESV) – "Charm is deceitful, and beauty is vain, but a woman who fears the Lord is to be praised."

God, I praise you for how Your grace has helped me heal from my past marriage and given me hope in a new marriage. I feel Your power most when I see my son actually run or stand on his tiptoes; when I see my husband who loves me, and every day when I come home.

I pray for wisdom in this difficult situation, knowing how to help Anthony in school so that he makes good decisions now for his future. Lord, let me lean on Your words, on Your will for my life, for Anthony's life. And I pray to be someone on whom Anthony, Dre, Stella, Carrie, Teyna, and LaTonya can lean on as well. I am stronger when I lean into You.

Saturday, January 26, 2019

John 10:27 – "My sheep listen to my voice; I know them, and they follow me."

God, I lift up this area of my life to the power of Your grace: My diet and my love for food.

Thank You for blessing me with just what I need when I thought I should have been elsewhere—You kept me at Durham for the right season. I pray to feel Your peace and joy when I struggle with food cravings, whether they are physical or mental. You have given me a spirit of love, joy, peace, patience, kindness, goodness, faithfulness, gentleness, and self-control. I have peace because I do not need the extra food. You are all the food and nourishment I need. Lord, transform me from the inside all the way out.

Tuesday, January 29, 2019

When I need a reminder of God's awesome power, I just look at Anthony's healing. God is alongside me every day. I am so grateful.

Saturday, June 8. 2019 (Here's where the PIVOT started showing up in my journaling.)

John 1:16 (GW) – "Each of us has received one gift after another because of all that the Word is."

Lord, Your grace fills me with hope for my PIVOT project, its success, and its distribution across the globe! Thank You for blessing me with just what I needed when I doubted myself. This is when You give me a verse, and another verse, and another. You always affirm me!

I pray for energy to bring Your light to this PIVOT vision and plan. Give me daily directions, the resources, the connections, and the knowledge to make this a reality so others can know that You are the HEALER for ALL people. You love people, and You are the only way someone can truly transform their life. Shower Your grace and joy on those in need, especially Dre, Anthony, Shellie Armstrong, Cindy Morrow, Summer K, Kassie Shaw Carley, and Tonia. Let me be Your light at 191 Beale Street. Let me be your light to my family.

Embolden me to approach my husband with grace. I want him to LIVE! Find a hobby. Find how You want to use him. I'm certain You did not gift him with so many talents and gifts for him to waste his time. And I know he is naturally shy, but Lord, I need him to talk more. Help me to be graceful in my approach. I pray my natural boldness is never mistaken for arrogance or selfishness.

Monday, June 24, 2019

Matthew 6:33 – "But seek first his kingdom and his righteousness, and all these things will be given to you as well."

This is the "P" verse for PIVOT! It is the number 1 reason why I say we must do this every morning, first thing.

Today I pray for discernment concerning my job. You know I love my job, but Dre wants me to actively seek something with more money. I pray that I do what YOU want me to do. If you say "move," I will move. Until then, I will do the work before me to the best of my knowledge and ability. I will use it as my stepping stone.

Lord, thank You for keeping me safe and calm – full of JOY! I may not always be happy, but I am completely satisfied.

Saturday, August 17, 2019

P – Lord, you are awesome! You have prepared, planned, set aside, made a way, and have brought me to this exact place – sitting in my prayer room, studying Your Word about being financially responsible and prepared.... In AWE that You are entrusting me with Your PIVOT plan! Wow! I am thankful, grateful, and so honored to take this plan to the world. Help me, Lord, to go where I need to go. Help me move where I need to move to find those who need You in their daily lives. Help me coach with expertise, my knowledge, and with authority on how women can have a personal relationship with You. Direct my thoughts so they will lead to productive and fruitful actions.

Give me patience and peace. I will not be overwhelmed. Take this illness inside of me and send it away! Bind up whatever harmful bacteria has come into my body and get rid of it! My health, my time, my energy, my resources will only be spent, Lord, on Your desires for me!

Father, I pray for Dre – that this week, provide restoration for him emotionally and mentally. Father, I know You are preparing multiple job offers for him now. I pray for those to move forward this week—that they present themselves to Dre and me, and that they will exceed our expectations and provide the support we need to live the plan that will honor You, that will share Christ with others and grow Your Kingdom on earth.

Thank You, Father!

Father, I pray for continued protection and guidance for Anthony. Thank You for preparing him for adulthood. I pray that his desire to go into the military will align with your plans—but if it does not, Lord, I know that he will still be okay. Whatever is Your will—I pray that!

I pray for a paid writing opportunity. I pray for an opportunity to learn how to write programs, etc.

I pray for an offer to adjunct.

I pray for a windfall of resources that allow me to create a financial strategy that provides—that allows for adventure and travel, that allows me and Dre to build our businesses in Your honor.

Finally, Father, I pray for a mentor or a coach to adopt me and help me become a paid writer, blogger, content creator, publisher, conference and retreat planner, and speaker.

I ask in Your holy name for all these things—and Lord, I pray I am a good, good steward to all these gifts, in Your name, for Your glory. Amen.

I – Learning a new podcast app.

V – Embracing a new 40-day money challenge and visualizing how much more disciplined I'll be on day 41.

T – Floor exercises today.

Sunday, August 18, 2019

P – The sword of the Spirit.

"God's Word" – an offensive weapon that requires warriors to know the Word to stand firm against our enemy.

Shelley, if you are not in your Bible every day, you are not maintaining the sharpness of your Bible.

God's Word ALONE holds the power and authority to gain the victory.

I – Investigate

Today, I'm looking at my website build, looking up best practices for a website, how to buy a domain, how to use it on my website, and launch. Also, I want to research 40-day financial plans to possibly do a 40-day PIVOT on my finances.

V – Here's what I'm claiming for the remainder of 2019:

- Website completed and in working order by November 1.

- Monetize a 40-day challenge.

- A 10-day PIVOT challenge.

- Completed two certifications online.

- Children's books available online.

- By November, I will be bringing in $400 through the PIVOT website and $700 in December.

In 2020, I see:

- Clients referring clients.

- Completed certification through the Christian Life Counseling School.

- I see residual income every month from $500 to $1000+ monthly.

- I see a successful launch party.

- I see a chamber membership for networking.

- I see a summer intern who will create a marketing campaign with graphic design updates.

- I see my first local women's conference.

- I see a retreat package with women traveling in to learn how to coach themselves, to implement a routine that renews them daily, transforms their minds to the thoughts of our Heavenly Father, and a plan of purpose that takes them into a successful and rewarding future.

- I see Dre and I in Belize again!

- I see meeting new potential clients while in Europe.

- I see retreats being planned in 2021 and 2022 in France, Italy, and London.

Saturday, September 14, 2019

P – Psalm 119:105 (ESV) *"Your word is a lamp to my feet and a light to my path."*

PIVOT is a reflection of the power of prayer and how a relationship with You brings peace and security. It's a reminder to me of Your unending love for me, for Dre, and for my son. You have blessed me with such a wonderful life—with a husband who is strong and complements me; with a son who is better than me in so many ways; You've given me my dream job, and I have friends who support me.

My faith grows stronger with every day that I am still at the Grizzlies, and every day I am married to Dre. Keep me faithful—knowing that I am right where I belong. Move me forward in my marriage, with the PIVOT book and its message, with my preparation and support for Anthony, and my work as a mentor.

Thursday, September 26, 2019

One year ago, today, we woke up in the hospital after Anthony's surgery. PRAISE GOD for those surgeons, the medical team, and the paramedics from Bartlett. Praise God for my hero, Andre, and praise God for this gift of healing for my son!!

I will never stop praising You for what You have done, Lord!

Today's verse is 1 Corinthians 15:58 (GW)

"So, then, brothers and sisters, don't let anyone move you off the foundation (of your faith). Always excel in the work you do for the Lord. You know that the hard work you do for the Lord is not pointless."

Lamentations 3:25 (NKJV)

"The Lord is good to those who wait for Him, to the soul who seeks Him."

I – Topic today is "active waiting."

A natural response to active waiting should be praising and worship. What does this really look like?

- Singing

- Arms outstretched

- Praying

- Knees on the ground

- Serving

- Palms up, hands open

See Romans 12:1

When we worship, we take our eyes off our problems and we set our hearts and minds on God.

Worship shifts our focus while we're in our waiting season to God. It's then we can see God's goodness, and a heart that is grateful for all He's done and will do.

Worship with your words, your thoughts, and your actions.

Thursday, January 28, 2021

P – Proverbs 31:15 – *"She gets up while it is still night; she provides food for her family and portions for her servant girls."*

I – This morning, I will investigate the marketing maven recommended by Shelley B. at yesterday's Sauce Marketing.

V – Putting my 2021 vision on paper in a diagram this morning.

O – I've promised myself to follow through on The PIVOT Project, the Pandemic Pearls art exhibition, and getting my Ed.D. To demonstrate my commitment, today I will get back to New Memphis for my Intern position.

T – Tomorrow is the Peloton delivery. Today—set up the space!

Tuesday, March 30, 2021

P – Romans 5:8 – *"But God demonstrates his own love for us in this: While we were still sinners, Christ died for us."*

This morning's prayer is one of thankfulness and blessings, Lord. Father, thank You for allowing me to get through yesterday's procedures with no incident. Thank You for my health. Thank You for my son, who stayed awake to take care of me. Thank You for gifting me with a husband who has been supportive and who sees my discomfort. Thank You for our sweet dog, Chelsie, who just brings us joy throughout our day. Thank You for the laughter You sent yesterday with the two nurses, for Shelley, my anesthesiologist, and for red toolboxes in the operating room. Bless all of these people today; give them Your reassurance that how they serve others is important work, and the work and service they do—they do it and it pleases You. Thank You, Lord!

I – Reviewed local health magazines for contacts to use for writing a Pandemic Pearl article.

V – Here's what I see, Father. Bless it. Edit it as You desire; enlarge it, and give me the fortitude, the resilience, and the resources and tools to make it happen!

- Pandemic Pearls Art Exhibition, March 2022

- Art posted in a local coffee shop, restaurant, or business.

- Dr. Kemp as of 2023!

- Liberty U will accept 6 hours of transfer credit.

- Retirement from the Grizzlies at 60 to run my own consulting business, including author, speaker, artist, coach.

- Author of The PIVOT Project, signed with a major publisher who will republish my children's books and does nine more (making a dozen), + PIVOT journals + PIVOT retreats.

- People all over the world seeing and experiencing Jesus through my work.

I – Reviewing the writer's conference notes and preparing the draft for submission—my proposal.

T – Walking Day!!

Idea today! "The PIVOT Circle"—a group of women who want to be part of the conversation—whatever it is—to pivot to a solution.

Tuesday, June 22, 2021

P – John 13:35 *"By this everyone will know that you are my disciples, if you love one another."*

Lord, You are THE ONE TRUE AND ONLY GOD—the same God who showered the kings of Israel, who gave mercy and who disciplined Your children. You were there when Elijah challenged the lovers of Baal and You were there when he prepared the bull as an offering and proof of Your love, Your very existence! Thank You for sharing this story with me today.

Just as Lysa has prompted me, show me where I place any self-reliance or any idols, when I should be focusing on You, Lord. Help me to always get better and become more like Jesus and less like me. My clothes! Clean out these pieces I don't even wear! Love them for the purpose they once had and then gift them to someone else who will need and love them now.

Father, help me to stay motivated for this Ed.D. program, to complete the proposed PIVOT Routine, and help me manage my time in the manner that is perfect timing for the acceptance of my manuscript, as well as Your vision for taking the pivot to people all over the world. How do I get this word out?

How do I get the right number of people to participate in my study?

And what specifically should I measure?

This research will bring You to and in front of business folks seeking a better way. Seeking YOU. Fill me with whatever is necessary to bring this routine to life. Lord, thank You for using me. I pray for Your hand in all things—to guide every move I make—for Your glory, God. In Jesus's name I pray. Amen.

I – Bible study today..... 1 Kings 17, 18

V – See prayer....

The PIVOT Project

Routine - Pandemic Pearls - Workshops - Workbook - 30-Day Devotionals

O – Today, I am going to open up the website and craft a new blog subject.

T – Peloton workout

Friday, December 22, 2023 – Food Day!

Yesterday was a success! Did I feel weak? Yes, but I think it's because I'm coming down with a sinus infection.

P – Philippians 3:13b-14 – *"But one thing I do: Forgetting what is behind and straining toward what is ahead, I press on toward the goal to win the prize for which God has called me heavenward in Christ Jesus."*

I – Spend 15 minutes looking at grants.

V – Used on the Envision app. Visualized walking the Grand Canyon at the age of 55.

O – Today, I'm giving up snacks, sweets, and time, so that I can clean and put away clothes. For the glory of God and to appreciate my home.

T – 30-minute walk with Cookie after work.

Friday, December 29, 2023

Down 5.81lbs.

My willpower was strong yesterday. I was at work alone, so that part was easy, but by 5 p.m. I was feeling hungry. Yet, I still stayed on plan.

P – Proverbs 23:7 (NKJV) – *"For as he thinks in his heart, so is he."*

We become what we think.

Romans 12:2a – *"Do not conform to the pattern of this world, but be transformed by the renewing of your mind."*

I – Read some more today on employability.

V – Focused on getting 15+ lbs off by the time I leave for Sarasota, then coming back and getting into the 190s, then 180s before Valentine's Day.

O – Giving up snacks today, not giving into my cravings, knowing that my hunger pains are really just my body resetting itself, preparing for a new set-point. My metabolism is increasing.

T – 15-minute Peloton, 10-minute core, 10-minute lower body strength.

Monday, October 23, 2023

God's wellness plan for all humankind:

- To be holy (producing fruit of the Spirit)

- To be whole (health in heart, mind, and body)

So that you will be fully alive, a living testimony to God's goodness and faithfulness. How is God's plan different than mine?

- Moderation in foods
- More pure/whole foods, like fruits and vegetables
- Less alcohol
- More walking
- More meditation and quiet time
- More time with God, Our Father
- Play
- Instead of ten cookies, it's one.
- Small bowl of chips and dip instead of a large one.

P – Matthew 5:16 – *"In the same way, let your light shine before others, that they may see your good deeds and glorify your Father in heaven."*

Shelley, keep doing what you're doing. Keep speaking about PIVOT. Keep searching for connecting mindfulness with God's wellness plans for you and others. Make a plan to continue giving your testimony away to others.

Your career, your experiences, your knowledge, your lessons, these are ALL your testimony, and they allow others to see your light and see God's power and positioning in your life.

I – It's a podcast day!

V – Starting next year's vision board. Incorporate more phrases next year so I can repeatedly say them to myself.

O – Giving up 30 minutes of TV after work for a walk.

T – My walk!

Tuesday, October 31, 2023

I listened to a podcast this morning on "The Art of Sufficiency."

Even when you have some success in weight loss or exercise or simply eating healthier, keep your mind and heart focused on God—NOT the food or the numbers on the scale or the exercise. As soon as you think you have arrived at the goal and have it under control, pride develops, which leads to rebellion.

Day by day, glory by glory, faith by faith.... We must continue to sow the good seeds of physical, emotional, mental, and spiritual health.

Physical exercise improves our fitness and our strength. Remembering who God is renews our minds and increases our joy.

Ah ha! THIS is why mindfulness is not about emptying your brain of all thoughts! It's really about training your mind to move out all of the head trash so that you can easily bring your mind and thoughts to God and His glory!!! When we can do this, we can renew our minds and experience joy!

P – Matthew 11:30 – *"For my yoke is easy and my burden is light."*

The enemy wants to create real and imagined obstacles to keep me from following God and to convince me that He is not good.

What real or imagined obstacles are keeping me from knowing God?

When you struggle because things feel hard, what will you do? Do you lean in? Do you press on? Do you pause? Do you turn and find another way? Or do you quit?

Shelley, God will ensure that you come face-to-face with what frightens you!

This is His way of showing you that fear has always been an illusion—projecting onto the walls of your unbelieving. Do not be afraid!

Hold your plan *loosely* so you are allowing God to lead your way. A God-centered plan keeps the will of God as the goal—NOT losing a certain number of pounds or getting into a certain suit for the day. Any plans we make that move ahead of God, or any work we do without the approval of God will lack His provision.

Lord – God – Father,

Thank You for protecting my morning time with You today! My days are lost—chaos—when I don't have my time with You each morning to center me. Father, thank You for the Bible study just completed in wellness. I see where I lacked in my previous attempts and plans to lose weight. I held too tightly to my plans, to my goals, and my goals were self-centered (as usual). Forgive me for wanting something that may be Your will for me but for all the wrong reasons. Losing weight or gaining strength and flexibility is fine, a will to contribute to the Great Commission, but not if that is my only desire. My desire to be lean and healthy should not be more than my desire to fulfill Your work. Forgive me, Lord!

I am so vain.

I am so self-centered.

I am confused.

And I took my eyes off You and turned them to myself. Forgive me! I pray that You continue to show me where I am failing so that I can change, so that I can rearrange my thoughts. Thank You for exposing me to mindfulness training. How can I take this training further to help others, Lord? How can I take what I have learned—and will continue to learn—plus my testimony and my faith in You to the world to fulfill Your work?

What do I want?

I want to use the tools You have gifted me with to teach people in the workplace a better way to work—to leave room for You in their work—to prioritize better. I want to talk to women and young adults about claiming a daily routine that will help them seek You every day and turn non-believers of Christ into believers!

I want to impact young people in a way that inspires them and motivates them to learn more about YOU so they can be saved, too. I want to be able to replace my current salary with money from books, journals, speaking tours, workshops, and conferences that will take me and Dre around the world. I want to use my money for the Kingdom's sake, not my own. My way is selfish and only effective for one person, but Your way is Christ's way and gives for MANY. THAT'S when I can feel satisfied about my money.

I want a happy and fulfilling marriage. I want to see laughter and joy in Dre. I want him to be used by You to the fullest, and I want him to impact men around the world with his knowledge and testimony about You.

I want Anthony to find his way with Your leading his heart and his mind. I want him to have an easier life than his dad's. Yes, I want him to go back to school. Yes, I want him to reach his full potential. Yes, I want him to meet his true love—a God-fearing girl who sees him as her one true love.

I want grandbabies.

I want family.

I want a home that is paid for and can become a central gathering place for family. I want to be Your voice, Your mouthpiece. And I never want to stop learning about You and Your Holy Spirit.

Through me, I want generations of believers to be born, to rise, and to take hold of the city of Memphis, of the U.S., and of communities all over the world. Lord, use me for Your amazing grace. Thank You for Your grace—Your love—Your oversight—Your direction—Your pruning—Your sufficiency—Your abundance—Your timing in all things. Help me to remember, Spirit, to include God in all my plans, to lean not into my own way of doing things. Help me to always ask, "How would You want me to do this?"

Lord, thank You for my time with You. May the words that come out of my mouth or out of my pen be pleasing in Your sight and to Your ears. Put people in my path today who need You and help me to give them Your light—our seasoning. Help me to add value while I'm at work and help me to accept that You are preparing now what will take me away from the Grizzlies. Thank You, Lord. It is in Your holy name I pray—Amen.

I – Podcast today – *Therapy and Theology* with Lysa TerKeurst

V – Affirmation day...

Today, I release the weight of self-made plans.

I no longer chase goals fueled by vanity or pressure—I pursue purpose.

God's yoke is easy. His burden is light.

I will not be distracted by fear, delay, or comparison.

The enemy may throw obstacles, but I will walk in the truth:

God is good. His plan is greater. And I trust Him with it all.

I am willing to let go of what makes me feel in control

so I can embrace what makes me more like Christ.

I welcome pruning. I welcome refining.

Because on the other side is freedom, impact, and generational purpose.

Today, I ask, "Lord, how would You want me to do this?"

And I listen with an open heart.

I choose Kingdom over comfort.

Discipline over distraction.

Faith over fear.

And joy over performance.

God is preparing me now for what's next.

And I'm ready.

O – Today I need more time to meditate and think about what is on my heart and in my mind. Today, I'm focusing on work—God's work and Grizzlies' work. Fasting while at work. Only broth. Clear body. Clear mind.

T – Peloton app. 5-minute warm-up. 5-minute Triangle Pose yoga. 5-minute Sphinx Pose. 5-minute Savasana. 5-minute cool-down. That made 25 minutes!

Saturday, April 19, 2025

It's rare that I remember my dreams in full, but this morning I woke up with vivid detail from one that refused to fade. Naturally, I turned to ChatGPT—something we didn't even have access to just five years ago—for insight. What a gift to have tools like this, right at our fingertips.

The Dream

After recently being let go from my job of seven years due to departmental restructuring, I've been in a season of both expected and unexpected transition. I had my suspicions that a layoff was coming, but the actual day still caught me off guard.

In the dream, my former boss handed me a beautiful brown leather razor. It was elegant, expansive—one that extended on both sides of the razor head, allowing for a wide, precise cut. It came tucked inside a matching soft, brown drawstring bag.

I asked ChatGPT to interpret it, and here's what it told me:

"The razor represents sharpness, cutting ties, or transformation. It may symbolize how suddenly and cleanly your job ended—but also the possibility of

renewal. The soft drawstring bag contrasts with the blade: nurturing, gentle, like protection around something painful but necessary. Together, they may suggest a bittersweet transition—one that was painful, yes, but also a gift."

When asked how I felt in the dream, I responded honestly: *"I was confused."*

And the reply was equally thoughtful:

"That confusion is important. It points to your heart and mind still trying to reconcile something that doesn't quite add up. Was the 'gift' helpful? Harmful? Unclear? Maybe the dream is nudging you to release what no longer serves you—and step into what has always been yours: your voice, your purpose, your calling."

I told ChatGPT about my work in Human Resources, and how for years I've also been writing and speaking—how my heart longs to do that full-time. Its response hit deeper:

"Then perhaps the razor wasn't a symbol of loss—it was a release. The bag? That's your intuition wrapping this sharp shift in care. Maybe it's time."

At first, it felt like confirmation. Like a divine "aha!" moment wrapped in algorithmic encouragement. But as the morning settled and my spirit leaned in, I felt something else.

A Holy Nudge

While the interpretation was comforting and even helpful, I was reminded: *my ultimate source is not AI. My trust cannot rest in technology, interpretations, or even the most well-meaning insights from others. My trust belongs to God alone.*

Proverbs 25:19 says:

"Like a broken tooth or a lame foot is reliance on the unfaithful in a time of trouble."

Anything other than God—even something as seemingly wise and insightful as ChatGPT—is ultimately flawed and finite. And while the tool may help us process or gain perspective, it should never replace our reliance on the Holy Spirit. Not our spouse, not a stranger online, and not a chatbot—however brilliant it may seem.

That doesn't mean we reject wisdom from others altogether. Scripture encourages community, counsel, and correction.

1 Corinthians 13:7 (ESV) – "Love bears all things, believes all things, hopes all things, endures all things."

Proverbs 27:5-6a – "Better is open rebuke than hidden love. Wounds from a friend can be trusted..."

But if I ever start reaching for AI before I reach for the Word... if I find myself consulting ChatGPT more than I consult my Creator—that's where the trouble lies. That's when reliance subtly shifts from reverence to replacement.

So, what now?

I've written down the dream. I've journaled the interpretations and dug for the lesson. And now, I offer it to you—the reader, the seeker, the one walking through your own shift. AI tools are incredible. They are efficient, even insightful. But let us never forget our foundation. Our source. Our Savior.

God is good. He was good while I worked in my dream job for over seven years.

He is good now, as I sit in my home office, asking, "What's next?"

And He will be good tomorrow, when the next chapter unfolds.

The razor may have symbolized a cut—but from a Kingdom perspective, it's a pruning. And God only prunes what He plans to grow.

So, here's to the tools, but even more to the truth.

Happy Easter Saturday. Amen.

Additional Journaling Prompts

1. What specific goal would you like to visualize achieving?

   ____

   ____

   ____

2. How do you want to feel when you've accomplished this goal?

   ____

   ____

   ____

3. What does success look like to you? How can you picture that in your mind?

   ____

   ____

   ____

4. Can you imagine what your environment looks like when you're achieving this goal? What sounds do you hear around you?

____

____

____

5. What physical sensations do you associate with your success? (e.g. energy, calmness, strength)

____

____

____

6. If you were to step into that moment, what would you see, hear, and feel?

____

____

____

7. What obstacles do you foresee, and how could you mentally rehearse overcoming them?

____

____

____

8. Can you visualize a time when you were faced with a challenge and how you successfully handled it?

____

____

____

9. How does it feel in your body when you imagine yourself succeeding?

____

____

____

10. What emotions come up when you see yourself achieving this goal in your mind?

____

____

____

11. How can you use these positive emotions as motivation to keep going when things get tough?

____

____

____

12. What time of day would be best for you to set aside a few minutes to practice visualization?

____

____

____

13. How can you make visualization a regular part of your routine?

____

____

____

14. What small steps can you take to begin visualizing daily?

15. How can you use visualization to reinforce the small actions that will get you closer to your goal?

16. What specific behaviors can you visualize yourself doing that will lead you to your desired outcome?

17. Can you recall a past experience where you succeeded or felt confident? How can you use that memory to fuel your visualization?

18. What would it feel like if you saw yourself achieving this goal with complete confidence?

19. How do you imagine your life will change once you've consistently visualized and worked toward your goal?

____

____

____

20. How can your visualizations today shape the future you're aiming for?

____

____

____

WORKS CITED

Achor, Shawn. *The Happiness Advantage: The Seven Principles of Positive Psychology That Fuel Success and Performance at Work*. Crown Business, 2010.

Alpine Skiing. "From Prodigy to Legend: Mikaela Shiffrin's Journey to 100 World Cup Wins." *FIS*, 28 Nov. 2024, https://www.fis-ski.com/alpine-skiing/news/2024-25/from-prodigy-to-legend%3A-mikaela-shiffrin-s-journey-to-100-world-cup-wins. Accessed 2 Nov. 2025.

Andrade, Chittaranjan, and Rajiv Radhakrishnan. "Prayer and Healing: A Medical and Scientific Perspective on Randomized Controlled Trials." *Indian Journal of Psychiatry*, vol. 51, no. 4, 2009, pp. 247–253, https://doi.org/10.4103/0019-5545.58288.

"Eliud Kipchoge Becomes First Athlete to Run a Marathon in Under Two Hours." *BBC Sport*, 12 Oct. 2019, https://feeds.bbci.co.uk/sport/live/athletics/49771509?page=2. Accessed 2 Nov. 2025.

Brooks, Arthur C. "The Type of Love That Makes People Happiest." *The Atlantic*, 11 Feb. 2021, https://www.theatlantic.com/family/archive/2021/02/falling-in-love-wont-make-you-happy/617989/. Accessed 4 Oct. 2025.

Bryant, Kobe. *The Mamba Mentality: How I Play*. MCD/Farrar, Straus and Giroux, 2018.

Coach Ashworth. "Basketball Passing Drill - PIVOT PASSING." *YouTube*, 2022, https://www.youtube.com/watch?v=3eacbv3pcaw.

Diaz, Keith. "Rx for Prolonged Sitting: A Five-Minute Stroll Every Half Hour." *Columbia University Irving Medical Center*, 12 Jan. 2023, https://www.cuimc.columbia.edu/news/rx-prolonged-sitting-five-minute-stroll-every-half-hour.

Djokovic, Novak. *Serve to Win: The 14-Day Gluten-Free Plan for Physical and Mental Excellence*. Zinc Ink, 2013.

Economo, Michael N., et al. "Learning and Control in Motor Cortex across Cell Types and Scales." *Journal of Neuroscience*, vol. 44, no. 40, 2 Oct. 2024, e1233242024. DOI: 10.1523/JNEUROSCI.1233-24.2024.

Fentuo, Tahiru Fentuo. "Tennis legend Serena Williams reveals her champion mindset: 'Be very disciplined.'" *The Olympic Games*, 27 June 2025, https://www.olympics.com/en/news/serena-williams-top-business-advice-discipline. Accessed 2 Nov. 2025.

Formica, Mark J. "The Science, Psychology, and Metaphysics of Prayer." *Psychology Today*, 28 July 2010, www.psychologytoday.com/us/blog/enlightened-living/201007/the-science-psychology-and-metaphysics-prayer. Accessed 13 May 2024.

Gallo, Carmine. "Michael Phelps Used This Mental Trick to Become the Greatest Olympian in History." *Forbes*, 1 June 2016, https://www.forbes.com/sites/levelup/2016/06/01/

todays-level-up-22-medals-3-habits-1-obsession-how-michael-phelps-reached-olympic-greatness/.

Gallo, Carmine. *The Storyteller's Secret: From TED Speakers to Business Legends, Why Some Ideas Catch On and Others Don't.* St. Martin's Press, 2016.

Gbadamosi, Rilwan. *Serena Williams: A Research Method and Psychological Perspective Study.* 24 Feb. 2020. DOI: 10.13140/RG.2.2.28716.62086.

Goleman, Daniel. *Emotional Intelligence: Why It Can Matter More than IQ.* Bantam Books, 1995.

Golliver, Ben. *Michael Jordan: The Life.* By Roland Lazenby, Little, Brown and Company, 2014.

Grover, Tim S. *Relentless: From Good to Great to Unstoppable.* Scribner, 2013.

Hölzel, Britta K., et al. "Mindfulness practice leads to increases in regional brain gray matter density." *Psychiatry Research: Neuroimaging*, vol. 191, no. 1, 2011, pp. 36-43.

Hood, James R. "Just five minutes of eccentric exercise a day can help your health, study finds." *Consumer Affairs,* 26 Mar. 2025, https://www.consumeraffairs.com/news/just-five-minutes-of-eccentric-exercise-a-day-can-help-your-health-study-finds-032625.html

Jackson III, Charles. "What Is Pivoting in Basketball?" *GCBC Basketball*, 23 Oct. 2023, www.gcbcbasketball.com/what-is-pivoting-in-basketball. Accessed 13 Feb. 2025.

Kipchoge, Eliud. *Eliud Kipchoge: Limitless: The Autobiography.* HarperCollins, 2021.

Lazenby, Roland. *Michael Jordan: The Life*. Little, Brown and Company, 2014.

Lipton, Bruce H. *The Biology of Belief: Unleashing the Power of Consciousness, Matter & Miracles*. Hay House, 2008.

Longman, Jeré. "Eliud Kipchoge Breaks Two-Hour Marathon Barrier." *The New York Times*, 12 Oct. 2019, www.nytimes.com. Accessed 30 Aug. 2025.

Mayberg, Helen S., et al. "Deep Brain Stimulation for Treatment-Resistant Depression." *Neuron*, vol. 45, no. 5, 2005, pp. 651–660, https://doi.org/10.1016/j.neuron.2005.02.014.

McGreevey, Sue. "Eight Weeks to a Better Brain." *The Harvard Gazette*, 21 Jan. 2011, https://news.harvard.edu/gazette/story/2011/01/eight-weeks-to-a-better-brain/.

Meier, Allison. "The Visualization Techniques of Champion Athletes." *Psychology Today*, 4 May 2024, www.psychologytoday.com. Accessed 13 Mar. 2025.

Mischel, Walter. *The Marshmallow Test: Mastering Self-Control*. Little, Brown and Company, 2014.

Mumford, George. *The Mindful Athlete: Secrets to Pure Performance*. Parallax Press, 2015.

National Academies of Sciences, Engineering, and Medicine. "Learning Is a Complex and Active Process That Occurs Throughout the Life Span, New Report Says." *The National Academies*, 4 Oct. 2018, https://www.nationalacademies.org/news/2018/10/learning-is-a-complex-and-active-process-that-occurs-throughout-the-life-span-new-report-says.

Nike. *Breaking2*. Nike, Inc., 2017.

Ohno, Apolo. *Hard Pivot: Embrace Change. Find Purpose. Show up Fully,* Center Street, 2022.

Outlaw, Kimberly R., and Mary S. Jackson. "Kobe Bryant: A Theoretical Approach to Understanding the Personal and Professional Life Trajectory of an Elite African American Athlete." *Journal of African American Studies*, vol. 25, no. 2, 2021, pp. 285–97. *JSTOR*, https://www.jstor.org/stable/48765858. Accessed 11 Dec. 2025.

Pangburn, Eric. "What Is A Pivot in Basketball? (Pivoting Techniques Explained)." *Info Hoops*, 19 Feb. 2023, https://infohoops.com.

Predoiu, Radu, et al. "Visualisation Techniques in Sport – the Mental Road Map for Success." *Discobolul – Physical Education Sport and Kinetotherapy Journal*, vol. 59, 30 Sept. 2020, pp. 245–256. DOI: 10.35189/dpeskj.2020.59.3.4.

Rashid, Zahid. "Stephen Curry Stats and Records: How Many Career Milestones Has the Warriors Icon Achieved?" *Pro Football Network*, 9 Mar. 2025, 12:22 p.m., https://www.profootballnetwork.com/nba/stephen-curry-stats-records-how-many-career-milestones-has-warriors-icon-achieved/

Reece, Andy. "The Importance of Prayer: 10 Reasons Why We Pray." *Christian.net*, 9 Jan. 2024, https://christian.net/resources/the-importance-of-prayer/.

Reece, Sandra. *Prayer and the Aligned Life: Finding Peace in God's Will.* GracePoint Press, 2024.

Ridley, James, director. *Kipchoge: The Last Milestone.* Ridley Scott Creative Group, 2021.

Rogers, Kristen. "The Psychological Benefits of Prayer: What Scientists Say about the Mind-Soul Connection." *CNN News*, 17 June 2020, https://www.cnn.com/2020/06/17/health/benefits-of-prayer-wellness.

Rose, Jordan. "What Is Pivoting in Basketball?" *Metroleague*, 15 Oct. 2023, https://www.metroleague.org/what-is-pivoting-in-basketball/.

Savitsky, Zach. "How to Run a Marathon in Under Two Hours: What We Learned from Eliud Kipchoge's 1:59 Attempt." *Science News*, 15 Aug. 2023, www.sciencenews.org/article/run-two-hour-marathon-drafting-pacers-eliud-kipchoge. Accessed 4 Oct. 2025.

Tardelli, Vitor S., et al. "Pressure Is Not a Privilege: What We Can Learn from Simone Biles." *Brazilian Journal of Psychiatry*, vol. 43, no. 5, Sept.–Oct. 2021, pp. 460–461. PubMed Central, https://www.ncbi.nlm.nih.gov/pmc/articles/PMC8555641/. Accessed 2 Nov. 2025.

Tare, Medha, et al. "The Science of Adult Learning: Understanding the Whole Learner." *Digital Promise*, 2020, https://digitalpromise.org/wp-content/uploads/2020/12/Adult-Learner-White-Paper-1.pdf.

Taylor, James. *Psyching for Sport: Mental Training for Athletes*. Human Kinetics, 1995.

USA Basketball. *The USA Basketball Coaching Guide for All Levels: Coaching Philosophy & Player Development Curriculum from the National Governing Body of Basketball*. USA Basketball, 2025.

Weg, Amber. "Simone Biles Shares the One Tool She Uses to Help Manage Her Anxiety." *Prevention.com*, 21 Nov.

2021, https://www.prevention.com/health/mental-health/a38291758/simone-biles-shares-tool-to-manage-anxiety/.

Williams, Blake. "Mastering Pivoting in Basketball: Essential Techniques and Drills for Game Success." *The Bruins Blog*, 30 June 2024, https://thebruinsblog.net/pivoting-in-basketball/.

Williams, Serena. *On the Line.* Grand Central Publishing, 2009.

HOW TO CONTACT THE AUTHOR

Thank you for reading *The PIVOT Principle*! I would love to hear how this book has impacted your life, leadership, or personal transformation journey. Whether you are interested in coaching, booking a speaking engagement, or simply want to share your story, I welcome your connection.

Dr. Shelley Kemp, Ed.D., SHRM-SCP

HR Professional **|** Author | Speaker | Coach | Founder, Pivot Well, LLC

Email: PivotRoutine@outlook.com

Website: www.shelleykemp.com

LinkedIn: linkedin.com/in/drshelleykemp

Speaking & Media Inquiries: PivotRoutine@outlook.com

I look forward to hearing from you. And remember—every pivot you make can lead to purpose, peace, and progress.

Connect with me on Instagram here: